1800 RIDDLES ENIGMAS AND CONUNDRUMS

DARWIN A. HINDMAN

DOVER PUBLICATIONS, INC.

NEW YORK

Published in Canada by General Publishing Company, Ltd., 30 Lesmill Road, Don Mills, Toronto,
Ontario.
Published in the United Kingdom by Constable
and Company, Ltd., 10 Orange Street, London WC 2.

1800 Riddles, Enigmas and Conundrums is a new
work, first published by Dover Publications, Inc., in
1963.

Standard Book Number: 486-21059-6
Library of Congress Catalog Card Number: 63-19492

Manufactured in the United States of America
Dover Publications, Inc.
180 Varick Street
New York, N.Y. 10014

Preface

The word *riddle* is used in this collection in a broad sense, as referring to a kind of puzzle—one in the form of a question that is blind, obscure, confusing, or misleading, and is intended to be guessed. If the riddle is based upon especially obscure or ambiguous allusions, it is called an *enigma*. If it is based upon a pun or other play on words, it is a *conundrum*. If the question is definitely intended to mislead, rather than to puzzle or confuse, it might be called a *catch* or *sell*.

The following collection includes some items that hardly conform to the above definition of a riddle. They are questions that are really not intended to be guessed, but intended only to prepare for the answer by the questioner himself. They are jokes or "wisecracks" rather than true riddles.

The collection makes no attempt to cover the broad and varied field of enigmas, including only a few of them. No riddle is omitted for the reason that it is old and well-known, and few are omitted for the reason that they are far-fetched or "corny."

I am grateful to Dr. Norman Lawnick and Miss Pat Harrington for reading the manuscript and making many valuable suggestions.

D.A.H.

Columbia, Missouri
January, 1963

Contents

1

Animals

BIRDS

Domestic Fowls

Why is a hen immortal?   *ANS: Because her son never sets.*

How can you keep a rooster from crowing on Monday morning?   *ANS: Eat him for Sunday dinner.*

Why is a chicken like a farmer?   *ANS: Because he delights in a full crop.*

Why would a compliment from a chicken be an insult? *ANS: Because it would be fowl language.*

Why did the farmer call his rooster "Robinson?"   *ANS: Because he crew so.*

What does a hen do when she stands on one foot?   *ANS: Lifts up the other.*

Why are a rooster's feathers always smooth?   *ANS: Because he carries a fine comb.*

How is a poultry dealer compelled to earn his living? *ANS: By fowl means.*

Why does a hen cross the road?   *ANS: To get to the other side.*

What did the little chick say when it found an orange in its nest?   *ANS: "Oh, look at the orange Mama laid."*

Why is a joke like a chicken?   *ANS: Because it contains a merry thought. ("Merrythought": The wishbone.)*

Why is a turkey like a ghost?   *ANS: Because he's always a-gobblin'.*

Why can hens lay eggs only in the daytime?   *ANS: Because at night they become roosters.*

Why don't fowls lay in the winter?   *ANS: Because there are no races on. ("Lay": To wager; bet.)*

Why should a fowl with only one wing and a fowl with two wings always disagree?   *ANS: Because there is a difference of a pinion between them.*

How can you tell the age of a hen?   *ANS: By the teeth.*

But hens do not have teeth.   *ANS: I mean by your own teeth.*

What is most like a hen stealin'?   *ANS: A cock-robin.*

Why is a goose like a cow's tail?   *ANS: Because it grows down.*

What does every duckling become when it first takes to water?   *ANS: It becomes wet.*

Why does a duck go into the water?   *ANS: For divers reasons.*

Why does he come out?   *ANS: For sun-dry reasons.*

Why does he go back into the water?   *ANS: To liquidate his bill.*

Why does he come out again?   *ANS: To make a run on the bank.*

If a man is on top of a monument with a live goose in his arms, what is the quickest way for him to get down?   *ANS: Pluck the goose.*

Three grown-up ducks and one baby duck were having a swim. Baby duck said, "Aren't we three having a good time?" Why did he say "three" instead of "four"? *ANS: Baby duck was too young to count.*

A duck before two ducks, a duck behind two ducks, and a duck between two ducks. How many ducks? *ANS: Three.*

A duck was swimming in a pond and a dog was sitting on its tail. How could that be? *ANS: The dog was on the shore, sitting on its own tail.*

If a peacock owned by you laid eggs in your neighbor's yard, who would own the eggs? *ANS: Eggs are laid by peahens, not by peacocks.*

Other Named Birds

Why should an owl be offended if you called him a pheasant? *ANS: Because you would be making game of him.*

What geometrical figure represents a lost parrot? *ANS: Polygon.*

Why is a crow the bravest of birds? *ANS: Because he never shows the white feather.*

Why is a crow? *ANS: Caws.*

What bird looks most like the stork? *ANS: The stork's wife.*

Why is the flight of an eagle a most unpleasant sight? *ANS: Because it's an 'igh soar.*

When is a pigeon like a drinking glass? *ANS: When it's a tumbler. (The tumbler is one of many varieties of domestic pigeon, other common varieties being pouter, carrier, homer, fantail, nun, jacobin, turbit, and trumpeter. The tumbler is so-called because of its habit of somersaulting backward in flight.)*

Any Bird

Why must birds in a nest always agree?   *ANS: To keep from falling out.*

Why do birds clean out a fruit tree so quickly?   *ANS: Because they take away a peck at a time.*

Why are birds melancholy in the morning?   *ANS: Because their little bills are all over dew.*

> Twice four and twenty blackbirds
> Were sitting in the rain;
> One shot killed a seventh,
> How many did remain?

ANS: The four that were killed; the other twenty-four flew away.

If you saw a bird sitting on a twig, how could you get the twig without disturbing the bird?   *ANS: Wait until the bird flew away.*

What Bird?

What bird moves in the highest circles?   *ANS: The eagle.*

What bird can lift the heaviest weight?   *ANS: The crane.*

What bird is most contented?   *ANS: The crow, for he never complains without caws.*

What bird is a girl's name?   *ANS: Eider, or Phoebe.*

What bird is easiest to deceive?   *ANS: The gull.*

What bird, found in Australia, has wings but cannot fly?   *ANS: A dead bird.*

What small bird is strong enough to overcome a man?   *ANS: Lark.*

What bird is run over the most?   *ANS: Rail.*

How do we know that one bird is insane?   *ANS: Because he's always a raven.*

What old bird is like a musical instrument?   *ANS: A peahen of forty (pianoforte).*

DOGS AND CATS

Dogs

Why is a dog's tail like the heart of a tree?   *ANS: Because it is farthest from the bark.*

Why is a dog biting his own tail a good manager?   *ANS: Because he makes both ends meet.*

When is a dog's tail not a dog's tail?   *ANS: When it's a-waggin'.*

If a dog should lose his tail, where would he go to get another?   *ANS: To Sears and Roebuck, where everything is retailed.*

Why is a dog's tail like an old-time expressman?   *ANS: Because it keeps a-waggin'.*

Why is a lame dog like a boy adding six and seven?   *ANS: Because he puts down three and carries one.*

When is a yellow dog most likely to enter a house?   *ANS: When the door is open.*

Why is a child's very young dog like the child's doll?   *ANS: Because it's a pup-pet.*

Why is a dog dressed warmer in summer than in winter?   *ANS: Because in winter he wears a fur coat, while in summer he wears a coat, and pants.*

What makes a coach dog spotted?   *ANS: His spots.*

When does a black dog change color in the moonlight?
ANS: When he turns to bay.

August was a hound pup who was always jumping at conclusions. One day he jumped at the conclusion of a stubborn mule. The next day was the first of September. Why?
ANS: Because that was the last of August.

When a doctor operates on a dog and comes to his lungs,
what does he find?   *ANS: The seat of his pants.*

"George, why is Rover like a formally proclaimed doctrine?"
ANS: "Because he's a dog, Ma."

Why is a dainty lap dog like a galloping hyena?   *ANS: Because he's a fastidious (fast hideous) beast.*

Why is a dog in a refrigerator like a telephone pole?   *ANS:
Because he's purp-in-de-cooler.*

Why is an ill-fed dog like a philosopher?   *ANS: Because
he's a thin cur.*

How can you keep a dog from going mad in August?   *ANS:
Shoot him in July.*

When is a black dog not a black dog?   *ANS: When he's a
grey-hound.*

Why is a man riding fast up a hill like another man taking
a young dog to a lady?   *ANS: Because he's taking a gallop
up.*

A hunter and his dog went out hunting. The dog went not
behind, went not before, nor on one side of the hunter.
Where did he go?   *ANS: On the other side.*

Why is a watchdog longer at night than in the daytime?
*ANS: Because he is let out every evening and taken in every
morning.*

What animal is more wonderful than a counting dog?
ANS: A spelling bee.

Why is a lame dog like a blotting pad?   *ANS: A lame dog is a slow pup; a slope up is an inclined plane; and an ink- lined plane is a blotting pad.*

Cats

When is a kitten like a teapot?   *ANS: When you're teasin' it.*

Why is a cat like a transcontinental highway?   *ANS: Be- cause it's fur from one end to the other.*

Why is a cat on her hind legs like a waterfall?   *ANS: Be- cause she is a cat-erect.*

Why does a cat sleep more comfortably in summer than in winter?   *ANS: Because summer brings the cat-er-pillar.*

What is most like a cat's tail?   *ANS: A kitten's tail.*

What do people in Tennessee call little gray cats?   *ANS: Kittens.*

Why are tomcats like unskillful surgeons?   *ANS: Because they mew-till-late and destroy patience.*

Why does a cat, when she enters a room, look first on one side, and then on the other? *ANS: Because she can't look on both sides at the same time.*

Why is a black cat looking out of the window of a corner house like an orange?   *ANS: Because it looks 'round.*

What has a head like a cat, feet like a cat, a tail like a cat, but isn't a cat?   *ANS: A kitten.*

Prove that a cat has three tails.   *ANS: No cat has two tails. One cat has one more tail than no cat. Therefore one cat has three tails.*

A room with eight corners had a cat in each corner, seven cats before each cat, and a cat on every cat's tail. How many cats were in the room?   *ANS: Eight.*

Two cats on opposite sides of a sharply sloping roof are about to slip off. Which will hold on longer?   *ANS: The one with the higher* mu. *(The Greek letter* mu *is the symbol for the coefficient of friction.)*

HORSES AND MULES

Why is a well-trained horse like a benevolent man?   *ANS: Because he always stops at the sound of whoa.*

What is the principal part of a horse?   *ANS: The mane part.*

Why is a colt like an egg?   *ANS: Because it can't be used until it is broken.*

Why does a piebald pony never pay toll?   *ANS: Because his master pays it for him.*

How can one put a horse on his mettle?   *ANS: Shoe him.*

How can you make a slow horse fast?   *ANS: Tie him up.*

How else can you make a slow horse fast?   *ANS: Stop feeding him.*

Why is a person approaching a candle like one about to get off a horse?   *ANS: Because he is going to a light.*

What horse can see behind as well as in front?   *ANS: A blind horse.*

Why should one never gossip in a stable?   *ANS: Because all horses carry tails.*

Why should a colt avoid exposure?   *ANS: Because he might take cold and become a little hoarse.*

What is wrong with describing an animal as a cart horse?
ANS: That is getting the cart before the horse.

Why is a sidesaddle like a four-quart measure?   *ANS: Because it holds a gal on.*

Why is a horse a curious feeder?   *ANS: Because he eats best when there isn't a bit in his mouth.*

How is it that a horse has six legs?   *ANS: He has forelegs in front and two legs behind.*

Why is a distanced horse in a race like a man in a shady place?   *ANS: Because he is out of the heat.*

> Thirty-two white horses on a red hill;
> Now they stamp, now they champ,
> Now they stand still.

ANS: The teeth.

What would you do if you found a horse taking a bath in your bathtub?   *ANS: Pull the plug out.*

Why is a horse like a lollipop?   *ANS: Because the more you lick it the faster it goes.*

Why is a horse in the hunting field an anomaly?   *ANS: Because the better tempered he is the better he takes a fence.*

Why do milkmen have white horses?   *ANS: To pull their wagons.*

How could a horse be like a bird?   *ANS: Didn't you ever see a horse-fly?*

Why should a horse not wear a high stiff hat?   *ANS: Because it would give him a hoss-tile appearance. ("Tile": A stiff hat, especially a silk one.)*

Why can there never be a best horse in a race?   *ANS: Because there is always a bettor.*

How many legs has a mule if you call its tail a leg?   *ANS: Four.*

Why does a donkey eat thistles?   *ANS: Because he's an ass.*

FISH AND SHELLFISH

Why do goldfish always seem so well traveled?   *ANS: Because they all have been around the globe.*

What is the best way to keep fish from smelling?   *ANS: Cut off their noses.*

Why should fish be well educated?   *ANS: Because they are commonly found in schools.*

Why should a fisherman always be wealthy?   *ANS: Because all his profit is net profit.*

What part of a fish is like the end of a book?   *ANS: The fin is.*

When is a wall like a fish?   *ANS: When it is scaled.*

Who caught the fossil fishes?   *ANS: The geological fissures.*

When are you closely related to a fish?   *ANS: When your grandmother is a good old soul.*

A man bought two fish, but when he got home he had three. How was this?   *ANS: He had two flounders—and one smelt.*

What fish has its eyes closest together?   *ANS: The smallest fish.*

In what very surprising places can you find fish?   *ANS: You can find a perch in a birdcage, a skate in a sports-goods shop, and a sole on a shoe.*

Why is a man who lives above a fishmonger's shop like a busy, meddling fellow?   *ANS: Because he's over a fish-house (over-officious).*

Why are fish in a thriving state like fish made to imitate them?   *ANS: Because they are hearty fish all (artificial).*

Why did the lobster blush?   *ANS: Because he saw the salad dressing.*

Why is a lobster like a loaf of bread that has fallen overboard?   *ANS: Because it is bred in the sea.*

What kind of noise annoys an oyster?   *ANS: A noisy noise annoys an oyster.*

Why is an oyster an anomaly?   *ANS: Because he grows a beard without a chin, and you have to take him out of his bed to tuck him in. ("Beard": The gills of some bivalves, as the oyster. "Tuck in": To eat, especially to eat greedily.)*

INSECTS, WORMS, AND THE LIKE

Why is a flea like a long winter?   *ANS: Because he makes a backward spring.*

What is worse than finding a worm in an apple?   *ANS: Finding half a worm.*

What is smaller than a mite's mouth?   *ANS: What goes into it.*

What is the largest bug?   *ANS: Humbug.*

What are the largest ants?   *ANS: Giants.*

Is a bee good at argument?   *ANS: Yes, he always carries his point.*

What insect does a blacksmith manufacture?   *ANS: He makes the fire fly.*

Why can't flies see in the winter?   *ANS: Because they leave their specks behind in the summer.*

When did the fly fly?   *ANS: When the spider spied her.*

Why are some men like glowworms?   *ANS: Because they shine only when it is dark.*

What do bees do with all their honey?   *ANS: They cell it.*

Why is it that mosquitoes cannot annoy a man while he is asleep?   *ANS: Because they wake him up first, and then annoy him.*

Why can a bee not be trusted?   *ANS: Because it is a humbug.*

How do we know that mosquitoes are happy?   *ANS: They always sing at their work.*

In a certain part of South America the mosquitoes are so large that they sit on the logs and bark as people go by, and a good many of them weigh a pound. Can this be true? *ANS: Yes, they sit on the logs and on the bark, and a sufficiently large number of them would weigh a pound.*

Why is a bee-hive like a spectator?   *ANS: Because it is a bee-holder.*

How do mosquitoes show that they are religious?   *ANS: First they sing over you, and then they prey upon you.*

CATTLE, PIGS, SHEEP, AND GOATS

Can you tell me how long cows should be milked?   *ANS: In the same way as short ones.*

When does a cow change places with her keeper?   *ANS: When she bellows, for then she is a cow-heard.*

When is a cow not a cow? *ANS: When she is turned into a pasture.*

Which has more legs, a cow or no cow? *ANS: No cow; a cow has four legs, but no cow has eight legs.*

A cattle ranch in Texas is owned by a New York man and operated by his three sons. The name of the ranch is "Focus." Why? *ANS: Because it is where the sons raise meat (sun's rays meet).*

Why does a baby pig eat so much? *ANS: To make a hog of himself.*

Why is a pig in the house like a house afire? *ANS: Because the sooner it is put out the better.*

Why do Pennsylvania farmers build their pigsties between their houses and their barns? *ANS: For their pigs.*

When would a farmer have the best opportunity for overlooking his pigs? *ANS: When he had a sty in his eye.*

Why is a dead pig like a specimen of handwriting? *ANS: Because it is done with the pen.*

What makes more noise than a pig caught in a fence? *ANS: Two pigs caught in a fence.*

Why is a pig the most remarkable animal in the farmyard? *ANS: Because he is first killed and then cured.*

Why are sheep in their fold like letters written after supper? *ANS: Because they are all penned at night.*

Why do white sheep eat so much more than black ones? *ANS: Because there are so many more of them.*

If a farmer had twenty sick sheep and one died, how many would he have left? *ANS: Nineteen. (This riddle, of course, must be proposed orally, so that "twenty sick sheep" will naturally be interpreted as "twenty-six sheep.")*

When is a goat nearly? *ANS: When it is all butt.*

If a goat should swallow a rabbit, what would be the result? *ANS: A hare in the butter.*

Why does a cow go over a hill?   *ANS: Because she can't go under it.*

What is the most important use for cowhide?   *ANS: To hold the cow together.*

MISCELLANEOUS NAMED ANIMALS

How does a camel appear pugnacious?   *ANS: He always has his back up.*

Why is a mahout, when trampled on by his elephant, like a lobster?   *ANS: Because he's a crushed Asian. ("Mahout": The keeper and driver of an elephant.)*

Would you rather an elephant attacked you or a gorilla? *ANS: I'd rather he attacked the gorilla.*

Why is an elephant like an apple pie?   *ANS: Because there is a b in both.*

Why has the beast that carries the palanquin of the queen of Siam nothing whatever to do with the subject?   *ANS: Because it's her elephant.*

Why is a hunted fox like a Puseyite?   *ANS: Because he's a tracked hairy 'un (tractarian). (Puseyism and Tractarianism are alternative names for an important religious movement in the Church of England.)*

Why has the giraffe such a long neck?   *ANS: Because his head is so far from his body.*

Why does a giraffe eat so very little?   *ANS: Because he makes a little food go a long way.*

What is worse than a giraffe with a sore throat?   *ANS: A centipede with sore feet.*

What do hippopotamuses have that no other animals have?
ANS: Baby hippopotamuses.

Why is a mouse like hay?   *ANS: Because the cat'll eat it.*

If I should catch a newt, why would it surely be a small one?
ANS: Because it would be my newt.

When is a man like a snake?   *ANS: When he is rattled.*

Why should a certain kind of snake be a good storyteller?
*ANS: Because he gets off a rattling good thing in the shape
of a tail.*

What makes a squirrel run up a tree?   *ANS: Aw, nuts!*

Why should a turtle be pitied?   *ANS: Because his is a hard
case.*

Why is a whale like a water lily?   *ANS: Because it comes
to the surface to blow.*

A frog, a duck, and a skunk all went to town to see the
circus. Did they all get in or not?   *ANS: No. The frog got
in because he had a green back, and the duck got in because
he had a bill, but the skunk did not get in because all he
had was a scent, and it was a bad one.*

WHAT ANIMAL?

What animal doesn't play fair?   *ANS: Cheetah.*

What farm animal is a cannibal?   *ANS: The cow; she eats
her fodder.*

What animal never grows old?   *ANS: Gnu.*

What animal do you think of when you hear a fish story?
ANS: Lion.

What animal would you like to be on a cold day?   *ANS: A little otter.*

> If a well-known animal you behead,
> A larger one you will have instead.

ANS: Fox—ox.

Add half a score to nothing, and what animal does it make? *ANS: To O add X and get OX.*

What creature becomes healthier when beheaded?   *ANS: Whale—hale.*

What animal drops from the clouds?   *ANS: The rain, dear.*

What animal do you think the most of?   *ANS: Ewe (you).*

2

The Bible

WHERE, OR WHAT?

What are the smallest two things mentioned in the Bible? *ANS: The widow's mite and the wicked flee.*

Where is the game of tennis mentioned in the Bible? *ANS: Where Joseph served in Pharaoh's court.*

What is the sharpest tool mentioned in the Bible? *ANS: The Acts of the Apostles.*

Where is an automobile mentioned in the Bible? *ANS: Where Elijah went up on high.*

Where is the first mention of a theatrical business venture? *ANS: Where Eve appeared for Adam's benefit.*

Where is paper money mentioned in the Bible? *ANS: Where the dove brought the green back to Noah.*

Where is the first mention of pork in the Bible? *ANS: Where Ham was taken into the ark.*

Where are walking sticks mentioned in the Bible? *ANS: Where Eve presented Adam with a little Cain.*

Where is medicine mentioned in the Bible? *ANS: Where the Lord gave Moses two tablets.*

Where is the theater mentioned in the Bible? *ANS: Where Joseph left the family circle and went into the pit.*

Where is the cash-and-carry system mentioned in the Bible? *ANS: Where Joseph said, "All the days of my appointed time will I wait until my change comes."*

17

Where is a most unequal contest mentioned in the Bible? *ANS: Where a mustard seed sprang up and waxed a great tree. ("Wax": To get the better of; to beat soundly or badly.)*

Where is the game of baseball mentioned in the Bible? *ANS: In numerous places, including:*
  (a) *Genesis refers to the big inning (beginning.)*
  (b) *Eve stole first, and Adam stole second.*
  (c) *Adam and Eve were both put out.*
  (d) *Cain made a base hit.*
  (e) *Noah put the dove out on a fly.*
  (f) *King Solomon had a diamond.*
  (g) *Abraham made a sacrifice.*
  (h) *Moses made a run after he slew the Egyptians.*
  (i) *Moses shut out the Egyptians at the Red Sea.*
  (j) *Samson struck out often when he beat the Philistines.*
  (k) *Rebeccah walked to the well with the pitcher.*
  (l) *Noah apparently was a great curve-ball pitcher. He pitched the ark within and without, and no one could get on to his ark.*

WHO?

Who was the most popular actor in the Bible?   *ANS: Samson; he brought down the house.*

Who was the most successful physician in the Bible?   *ANS: Job; he had the most patience.*

Who was the first man mentioned in the Bible?   *ANS: Chap. One.*

What man in the Bible (beside Adam) had no parents? *ANS: Joshua, the son of Nun.*

Who first held land in his own name?   *ANS: Lot.*

Who was the fastest runner in the Bible?   *ANS: Adam; he was first in the human race.*

Who was the straightest man in the Bible?   *ANS: Joseph;*
Pharaoh made a ruler of him.

What king, mentioned in the Bible, was often in his contemporaries' mouths?   *ANS: Agag.*

What five Old Testament characters in one family, when
named, constitute an order that a boy be punished?   *ANS:*
Adam, Seth Eve, Cain Abel.

Who was the strongest man in the Bible?   *ANS: Jonah;*
the whale couldn't keep him down.

Who was the first electrician in the Bible?   *ANS: Noah;*
he made the ark light on Mt. Ararat.

Who were the three Tom Thumb apostles?   *ANS: Peter,*
James, and John; they all slept on a watch.

Who won the first horse race in the Bible?   *ANS: Herod-*
ias's daughter, when she got a head of John the Baptist on
a charger.

Who killed a fourth part of all the people in the world?
ANS: Cain, when he killed Abel.

Who was the first great financier in the Bible?   *ANS:*
Noah, he floated his stock while the whole world was in
liquidation.

What three noblemen are mentioned in the Bible?   *ANS:*
Barren fig tree, Lord how long, and Count thy blessings.

Who were the shortest men in the Bible?   *ANS: It is com-*
monly believed that they were Knee-high-miah and Bildad
the Shuhite; but it may have been St. Paul, for he said,
"Silver and gold have I none," and no one could be shorter
than that.

From the name of what king of Israel can you take six and
leave his father?   *ANS: David. Take VI from his name*
and leave Dad.

ADAM AND EVE

At what time of day was Adam born?   *ANS: A little before Eve.*

Why should Adam have been satisfied with his wife?   *ANS: Because she was cut out for him.*

What fur did Adam and Eve wear?   *ANS: Bare-skin.*

Why were Adam and Eve a grammatical anomaly?   *ANS: Because they were two relatives without an antecedent.*

Why had Eve no fear of the measles?   *ANS: Because she'd Adam.*

What was it that Adam never saw, never possessed, yet left two to each of his children?   *ANS: Parents.*

What did Adam first plant in the Garden of Eden?   *ANS: His foot.*

Why did Adam bite the apple that Eve gave to him?   *ANS: Because he had no knife.*

What did Adam and Eve do when they were expelled from the Garden of Eden?   *ANS: They raised Cain.*

How many apples were eaten in the Garden of Eden? *ANS: Eleven: Eve ate, and Adam too, and the Devil won.*

How do we know that Cain was an enemy of President Lincoln?   *ANS: Because he hated Abe-L.*

How did Adam and Eve feel when they left the Garden of Eden?   *ANS: Put out.*

For what corporation was Eve made?   *ANS: For Adam's express company.*

How long did Cain hate his brother?   *ANS: As long as he was Abel.*

Why were the gates of the Garden of Eden closed after Adam and Eve were expelled? *ANS: To keep the damned pair out.*

To what church did Eve belong? *ANS: Adam thought her Eve angelical.*

How were Adam and Eve prevented from gambling? *ANS: Their paradise (pair o' dice) was taken away from them.*

Who was the first man? *ANS: Adam.*

Well, who was the first woman? *ANS: Eve.*

Well, then, who killed Cain? *(The answer is likely to be "Abel.")*

What regiment was Adam in? *ANS: The Buffs. ("Buffs": The old third regiment of the line in the British army. "Buff": The bare skin.)*

NOAH AND HIS ARK

Where was Noah when the lights went out? *ANS: In d' ark.*

Where did Noah keep his bees? *ANS: In the ark hives.*

In what order did Noah come from the ark? *ANS: He came forth.*

Why could nobody play cards on the ark? *ANS: Because Noah sat on the deck.*

Why did not the worms, like other creatures, go into the ark in pairs? *ANS: Because they went in apples.*

Where did Noah strike the first nail in the ark? *ANS: On the head.*

Why was Noah like an unfortunate cat?   *ANS: Because it was forty days and forty nights before he saw Ararat (e'er a rat).*

Why didn't Noah catch more fish than he did while he was in the ark?   *ANS: Because he had only two worms.*

Which animal took the most luggage into the ark, and which ones took the least?   *ANS: The elephant took most, because he took a trunk; the fox and the cock took least, because they had only a brush and comb between them.*

Why do we suppose that Noah had beer in the ark?   *ANS: Because the kangaroo went in with hops, and the bear was always Bruin.*

MOSES AND THE CHILDREN OF ISRAEL

How do we know that Moses wore a wig?   *ANS: Because he was sometimes seen with Aaron and sometimes without Aaron.*

Why was Moses the wickedest man that ever lived?   *ANS: Because he broke all the ten commandments at once.*

Why did Moses lose the race?   *ANS: Because the Lord told him to come forth.*

When did Moses sleep five in a bed?   *ANS: When he slept with his forefathers.*

Why was Pharaoh's daughter like a skillful financier?   *ANS: Because she took a little prophet from the rushes on the banks.*

What did the Egyptians do when it got dark?   *ANS: They turned on the Israelites.*

What did the Children of Israel have to eat while they were in the desert?   *ANS: The sand which is there.*

Where did the material for the sandwiches come from? *ANS: Ham was sent there with his followers, who were bred and mustered, and when Lot's wife was turned into a pillar of salt, all but her (butter) went into the desert.*

How were the Egyptians paid for the goods taken by the Israelites on the night of their flight? *ANS: They received a check on the bank of the Red Sea.*

VARIOUS NAMED PEOPLE

Of what simple affliction did Samson die? *ANS: He died of fallen arches.*

What did Job's wardrobe consist of? *ANS: Three wretched comforters.*

Why was the prophet Elijah like a horse? *ANS: Because he was fed from aloft.*

Why was Balaam like a Life-Guardsman? *ANS: Because he went about with his queer ass (cuirass).*

Why was John the Baptist like a penny? *ANS: Because he was one sent.*

Where did the Witch of Endor live? *ANS: At Endor.*

What did Lot's wife turn to before she turned to salt? *ANS: She turned to rubber.*

Why ought one to be encouraged by the story of Jonah? *ANS: Because he was down in the mouth, but he came out all right.*

Who was Jonah's guardian? *ANS: The whale brought him up.*

Why was St. Paul like a horse? *ANS: Because he liked Timothy.*

How do we know that St. Paul was a cook?   *ANS: The Bible says he went to Philippi.*

What became of Lot when his wife was turned into a pillar of salt?   *ANS: He took a fresh one.*

Why was Lot's wife turned into a pillar of salt?   *ANS: Because she was dissatisfied with her Lot.*

In what way was Ruth very rude to Boaz?   *ANS: She pulled his ears and trod on his corn.*

If Solomon was the son of David, and Joab was the son of Zeruiah, what relation was Zeruiah to Joab?   *ANS: His mother. (Many persons will answer "his father," forgetting that Zeruiah was a woman.)*

What time of the year was it when the prodigal son came home?   *ANS: Winter. It must have been icy, for we are told that his father "went out and fell on his neck."*

MISCELLANEOUS BIBLE RIDDLES

If you became security at police court for a shady acquaintance, why would you be like the most extraordinary ass that ever lived?   *ANS: Because you would act the part of a donkey to bail 'im.*

Why did they not use slates and pencils in Bible times? *ANS: Because the Lord told them to multiply on the face of the earth.*

Why were the early rulers of Israel called Judges?   *ANS: Because they presided over a Jewry.*

In what way does a confidence man live up to Bible teachings?   *ANS: When a stranger comes along he takes him in.*

3

The Body, Its Parts and Its Ailments

THE BODY IN GENERAL

Why can two slender persons not become great friends?
ANS: Because they must always be slight acquaintances.

When is a man thinner than a lath?   *ANS: When he's a-shaving.*

What is the best way to get fat?   *ANS: Go to the butcher shop.*

What would tickle a fat man a great deal?   *ANS: A fly on his nose.*

Why should one not laugh at a fat man?   *ANS: Because one should never laugh at another's expanse.*

Why, when a fat man gets squeezed while coming out of an opera, does it make him complimentary to the ladies?
ANS: Because the pressure makes him flatter.

What happened to the fat woman who sat on a flagpole to reduce?   *ANS: She fell off.*

AILMENTS AND THEIR TREATMENT

Doctor, Dentist, and Drugs

When is a doctor most annoyed?   *ANS: When he is out of patients.*

What kind of doctor would a duck become?   *ANS: A quack doctor.*

Why is it wrong to call a dentist's room a dental parlor? *ANS: Because it is a drawing room.*

Why should a doctor be less likely than other people to be upset on the ocean?   *ANS: Because he is accustomed to see sickness.*

Why is a doctor the meanest man on earth?   *ANS: Because he treats you and then makes you pay for it.*

How do we know that a dentist is unhappy at his work? *ANS: Because he always looks down in the mouth.*

Why is a dead doctor like a dead duck?   *ANS: Because he has done quacking.*

Why wouldn't Mother let the doctor operate on Father? *ANS: Because she didn't want anybody else to open her male.*

Why should a fainting woman have more than one doctor? *ANS: Because if she is not brought to, she will die.*

What is the greatest surgical operation on record?   *ANS: Lansing, Michigan.*

Why is a tonic like an ambulance?   *ANS: Because you take it when you are run down.*

Why is a thief like an aspirin given to a woman?   *ANS: Because he's a pilferer (pill for her.)*

In what liquid does the Queen of England take her medicine?   *ANS: Inside her.*

What is the best thing to take when you are run down? *ANS: The number of the car that hit you.*

Why did the moron always walk tiptoe past the medicine cabinet?   *ANS: He didn't want to awaken the sleeping pills.*

Sickness, Injury, and Pain

What is the only pain of which one makes light?   *ANS: A window-pane.*

Why is an infirmity like a loose knot?   *ANS: Because it is a frail-ty.*

Of what disease would a duke prefer to die?   *ANS: Dropsy, because it is a swell disease.*

Why does your sense of touch suffer when you are ill?   *ANS: Because you don't feel well.*

Why would a sixth sense be a handicap?   *ANS: Because it would be a new sense.*

Why is a nail in an oak log like a sick person?   *ANS: Because it's in firm.*

A knight in shining armor had a pain. Tell me in one sentence when it was and where it was.   *ANS: It was in the middle of the night (knight).*

What makes everybody sick but those who swallow it?   *ANS: Flattery.*

Why is a woman when sick at sea like some of our literary men?   *ANS: Because she is a contributor to the Atlantic.*

Why may a dyspeptic hope for a long life?   *ANS: Because he can't di-gest yet.*

Why should a man with gout make his will?   *ANS: Because he will then have his legatees.*

Why is a bad cold a great humiliation?   *ANS: Because it brings the proudest man to his sneeze.*

What gives a cold, cures a cold, and pays the doctor?   *ANS: A draft.*

What is the latest prescription for seasickness?   *ANS: Bolt your food down.*

Why is a man with a cold on his chest not a man?   *ANS: Because he's a little hoarse.*

Why is measles like a steel trap?   *ANS: Because it is catching.*

Where is the best place to have a boil?   *ANS: On another fellow.*

When is a stormy, windy day like a child with a cold in its head?   *ANS: When it blows, it snows.*

THE HEAD AND FACE

Hair and Baldness

Why is a youth trying to raise a mustache like a cow's tail? *ANS: Because he grows down.*

Why does the hair on a man's head usually turn gray before his mustache does?   *ANS: Because it is about twenty-one years older.*

Why has man more hair than woman?   *ANS: Because he's naturally her suitor (hirsuter).*

What makes a man bald-headed?   *ANS: Want of hair.*

Why is a bald head like Paradise?   *ANS: Because there's no parting or dyeing there.*

Why does a bald-headed man have no use for keys?   *ANS: Because he has lost his locks.*

Why do women not become bald as soon as men?   *ANS: Because they wear their hair longer.*

Why has Timothy Moore, since he has lost his hair, become like one of our Eastern cities?   *ANS: Because he is bald Tim Moore.*

Why do women put their hair in rollers?   *ANS: To wake curly in the morning.*

Why does a youth injure his stature by encouraging the growth of whiskers?   *ANS: Because he begins to grow down.*

Other Parts of the Head and Face

Why isn't your nose twelve inches long?   *ANS: Because if it were it would be a foot.*

When is a nose not a nose?   *ANS: When it is a little reddish.*

What is the cheapest feature of the face?   *ANS: Nostrils; they are two for a scent.*

Why are your nose and your pocket handkerchief like deadly enemies?   *ANS: Because they seldom meet without coming to blows.*

Why is the nose in the middle of the face?   *ANS: Because it is the scenter.*

Why are your nose and your chin always at variance?   *ANS: Because words are continually passing between them.*

Why is a situation of great trust like a back tooth?   *ANS: Because it is hard to fill.*

Why can you not remember the last tooth that you had pulled?   *ANS: Because it went right out of your head.*

Why can a blind man see his father?   *ANS: Because his father is always a parent.*

What should you always do with your eyes?   *ANS: Dot them.*

What has five eyes, but cannot see?   *ANS: The Mississippi River.*

What is it that by losing an eye has nothing left but a nose?
ANS: The word NOISE.

How many persons can a deaf-and-dumb man tickle?   *ANS: He can gesticulate (jest tickle eight).*

What has fifty heads but can't think?   *ANS: A box of matches.*

Why are Panama hats like deaf people?   *ANS: Because you can't make them here.*

What are the little white things in your head that bite?
ANS: Teeth.

When is a young lady's cheek not a cheek?   *ANS: When it is a little pale.*

> Runs and runs but never walks,
> Has a long tongue but never talks.

ANS: A wagon.

ARMS AND LEGS

When do elephants have eight feet?   *ANS: When there are two of them.*

What has four legs and a back, but no body?   *ANS: A chair.*

What has four legs and only one foot?   *ANS: A bedstead.*

What is alive and has only one foot?   *ANS: A leg.*

What has four legs and feathers?   *ANS: A featherbed.*

What has a hundred legs but cannot walk?   *ANS: Fifty pairs of pants.*

What has four legs and flies?   *ANS: A dead horse.*

What else has four legs and flies?   *ANS: Two pairs of pants.*

What has eighteen legs and catches flies?   *ANS: A baseball team.*

What has four legs and flies in the air?   *ANS: Two birds.*

What has eight legs and sings very loud?   *ANS: A male quartet.*

> Three feet I have, but ne'er attempt to go,
> And many nails theron, but not one toe.

ANS: A yard measure. ("Nail": One-sixteenth of a yard, or 2 ¼ inches.)

If a man should break his knee, where would he go to get another?   *ANS: To Africa, where the Negroes.*

If a boy should lose his knee, where would he go to get another?   *ANS: To a butcher shop, where kid-neys are sold.*

What has a foot on each end and one in the middle?   *ANS: A yardstick.*

What did the big toe say to the little toe?   *ANS: "There's a heel following us."*

Why did the moron cut his fingers off?   *ANS: Because he wanted to write shorthand.*

When may a man be said to have four hands?   *ANS: When he doubles his fists.*

Why is your thumb, when you are putting on a glove, like eternity?   *ANS: Because it is ever last in.*

What do you call a man who doesn't have all his fingers on one hand?   *ANS: Perfectly normal, for his fingers are properly divided between his two hands.*

What has neither flesh nor bone, but has four fingers and a thumb?   *ANS: A glove.*

4

Clothing, Accessories, and Personal Adornment

COATS, TROUSERS, AND CLOTHING IN GENERAL

Why is swearing like a worn-out coat? *ANS: Because it is a bad habit.*

Why may a beggar wear a very short coat? *ANS: Because it will be long enough before he gets another.*

What is the best way to make pants last? *ANS: Make the coat and vest first.*

Which is the west side of a little boy's trousers? *ANS: The side the son sets on.*

If a good boy wears his pants out, what does he do? *ANS: He wears them in again.*

One morning a boy couldn't find his trousers; what did he do? *ANS: He raced around the room until he was breathing in short pants.*

Why did George Washington wear red-white-and-blue suspenders? *ANS: To hold his pants up.*

Why is a small boy who has ripped his pants on a nail like the preacher who is saying, "Finally, my brethren"? *ANS: Because he's tor'd his clothes (he's toward his close).*

Why is a person who buys his clothes on the installment plan dynamic? *ANS: Because everything he has on is charged.*

What does the evening wear?   *ANS: The close of day.*

What suit lasts longer than you want it to?   *ANS: A lawsuit.*

Why does a policeman have brass buttons on his coat? *ANS: To button up his coat.*

When may a man's coat pocket be empty and still have something in it?   *ANS: When it has a hole in it.*

Why does a coat get larger when it is taken out of a suitcase? *ANS: Because when you take it out you find it in creases.*

What is the correct uniform for a soldier?   *ANS: Right dress.*

What is always at the head of fashion, yet always out of date? *ANS: The letter F.*

HATS AND HOODS, SHOES AND HOSE

Why is a bad hat like a fierce snarling dog?   *ANS: Because its nap's awful.*

Why should a straw hat never be raised to a lady?   *ANS: Because it is never felt.*

What member of Congress wears the largest hat?   *ANS: The one with the largest head.*

When is a beaver hat a wide-awake?   *ANS: When it has lost its nap. ("Wide-awake": A low-crowned soft felt hat. Such a hat was part of the uniform worn by companies of young Republicans in the Presidential campaign of 1860.)*

Why does a miller wear a white hat?   *ANS: To cover his head.*

What is the ugliest hood ever worn?   *ANS: Falsehood.*

What is the difference between a sunbonnet and a Sunday bonnet?   *ANS: A day's difference.*

Why is it a mistake to wear a bedroom slipper?   *ANS: Because when you do you put your foot in it.*

What makes a pair of shoes?   *ANS: Two shoes.*

Which one of our Presidents wore the largest shoes?   *ANS: The one with the biggest feet.*

Why is it of no use to employ a barefooted messenger?   *ANS: Because he is sure to go on a bootless errand.*

When a shoemaker makes a shoe, what is the first thing that he uses?   *ANS: The last.*

When is a pair of shoes like a dying man?   *ANS: When the sole is departing from the body.*

When is a stocking like the first rule in dancing?   *ANS: When its toes are out.*

When you go to bed, why are your shoes like a deferred resolution?   *ANS: Because they are put off till the next day.*

Why is a size thirteen shoe like a noble-hearted, generous man?   *ANS: Because it has a large sole.*

When is a pair of stockings like a very old person?   *ANS: When they are on their last legs.*

When a little boy gets his stockings on wrong side out, what does his mother do?   *ANS: She turns the hose on him.*

Why is a garter like the gate of a slaughter house?   *ANS: Because it holds the stock-in'.*

DRESSES AND SKIRTS

When is an altered dress like a secret?   *ANS: When it is let out.*

When is a dress like an unfortunate bullfighter?   *ANS: When it is gored.*

What dress should a woman have to keep the rest of her wardrobe clean?   *ANS: A laun-dress.*

What is the latest thing in dresses?   *ANS: A nightdress.*

What kind of dress lasts longest?   *ANS: A housedress, for it is never worn out.*

Why is the latest thing in a fashionable gown like a South African bushman's club?   *ANS: Because it is perfectly stunning.*

Why is every woman extravagant in dresses?   *ANS: Because whenever she buys a new dress she wears it out on the very first day.*

What are men's opinions of riding skirts?   *ANS: They are divided.*

> Daffy-Down-Dilly has come to town,
>   In a yellow petticoat and a green gown.
ANS: A dandelion.

Who wears thirty-six petticoats and never had a dressmaker?   *ANS: An onion.*

ACCESSORIES AND ADORNMENT

What kind of umbrella does the President's wife carry on a rainy day?   *ANS: A wet one.*

Why is an umbrella a paradox?   *ANS: Because it is most useful when used up.*

Three large women went walking under one umbrella, but none of them got wet. Why?   *ANS: It wasn't raining.*

When is an umbrella like a convalescent person?   *ANS: When it is re-covered.*

Why is it illegal for a man to carry a short walking stick? *ANS: Because it can never be long to him.*

What kind of cravat would a hog be likely to choose? *ANS: A pigsty.*

What is the biggest jewel in the world?   *ANS: A baseball diamond.*

Why is attar of roses never moved without orders?   *ANS: Because it is scent wherever it goes.*

How can you make a pearl out of a pear?   *ANS: Add L to it.*

Why is a cannon like a vanity case?   *ANS: Because it is useless without powder.*

CLOTHING MATERIALS AND SUPPLIES

Appropriate Material

What is appropriate material for an artist to wear?   *ANS: Canvas.*

What is appropriate material for an athletic trainer to wear? *ANS: Rubber.*

What is appropriate material for a bald man to wear? *ANS: Mo'-hair.*

What is appropriate material for a banker to wear?   *ANS: Checks, or cashmere.*

What is appropriate material for a barber to wear?   *ANS: Haircloth.*

What is appropriate material for a baseball player to wear?
ANS: Batiste.

What is appropriate material for a dairyman to wear?
ANS: Cheesecloth.

What is appropriate material for a defeated team to wear?
ANS: Worsted.

What is appropriate material for an editor to wear?   *ANS: Prints.*

What is appropriate material for a fat man to wear?   *ANS: Broadcloth.*

What is appropriate material for a filling-station operator to wear?   *ANS: Oilcloth.*

What is appropriate material for a fisherman to wear?
ANS: Net.

What is appropriate material for a gardener to wear?   *ANS: Lawn.*

What is appropriate material for a hunter to wear?   *ANS: Duck.*

What is appropriate material for an inventor to wear?
ANS: Patent leather.

What is appropriate material for a jeweler to wear?   *ANS: Goldcloth.*

What is appropriate material for a musician to wear?   *ANS: Organdy.*

What is appropriate material for a sportsman to wear?
ANS: Outing flannel.

What is appropriate material for a tall man to wear?   *ANS: Longcloth.*

What is appropriate material for an undertaker to wear?
ANS: Crepe.

What is appropriate material for a yachtsman to wear?
ANS: Sailcloth.

Miscellaneous Materials and Supplies

Why is a well-worn piece of cloth like a sleepless person?
ANS: Because it has no nap.

What is the most seasonable material for a man's suit?
ANS: Salt and pepper.

What is a button?   *ANS: A small event that is always coming off.*

What goes around a button?   *ANS: A goat.*

CLOTHING WORKERS

How would you speak of a tailor when you did not remember his name?   *ANS: As Mr. Sew-and-Sew.*

What is the most important reason for not having an unskillful tailor?   *ANS: You get bad habits from him.*

When does a tailor serve his customers both well and ill?
ANS: When he gives them fits.

Why has the shoemaker wonderful powers of endurance?
ANS: Because he holds on to the last.

Why are washerwomen foolish people?   *ANS: Because they put out their tubs to catch soft water when it rains hard.*

Why is a washerwoman like Saturday?   *ANS: Because she brings in the clothes of the week.*

5

Food and Drink; Eaters and Drinkers

FOOD

Food in General; Hunger and Eating

How do you keep food on an empty stomach?   *ANS: Bolt it down.*

Why is food that does not agree with one like a cook's apron? *ANS: Because it goes against the stomach.*

Why is the food that one eats on an ocean liner like a difficult conundrum?   *ANS: Because one is obliged to give it up.*

What is the worst kind of fare for men to live on?   *ANS: Warfare.*

Why is a situation with no work required like a good dinner eaten by a convalescent?   *ANS: Because it's a sinecure.*

What is the best key to a good dinner?   *ANS: Tur-key.*

What would happen to a man if he swallowed his teaspoon? *ANS: He wouldn't be able to stir.*

What is eaten for breakfast or lunch, but usually drunk only for dinner?   *ANS: Toast.*

What articles of diet just escaped being flirts?   *ANS: Croquettes; without R they are coquettes.*

Why should a greedy man wear a plaid vest?   *ANS: To keep a check on his stomach.*

Is it safe to write a letter on an empty stomach?   *ANS: It is safe enough, but it is better to write the letter on paper.*

Which is better behaved, cake or wine?   *ANS: Cake, for it is only occasionally tipsy, while wine is always drunk. ("Tipsy cake": Cake saturated with wine and served with custard sauce.)*

What is the greatest instance of cannibalism on record? *ANS: When a rash man ate a rasher.*

Why did the moron eat dynamite?   *ANS: He wanted his hair to grow out in bangs.*

What is the greatest feat, in the eating way, ever known? *ANS: That of the man who bolted a door and then sat down and swallowed a whole story.*

If you were locked in a room with only a bed and a calendar, how could you survive?   *ANS: You could drink water from the springs in the bed, and eat dates from the calendar.*

Pastry

What becomes of the chocolate cake when your hungry son eats it?   *ANS: It vanishes into the empty heir.*

In what country were the first doughnuts fried?   *ANS: In Greece.*

Why is bread like the sun?   *ANS: Because it rises in the yeast and sets in the vest.*

What is the best thing to put into pies?   *ANS: Your teeth.*

What will make pies inquisitive?   *ANS: S will make spies of them.*

Why is a mince pie like a meeting house?   *ANS: Because you can walk into it. ("Walk into": To eat greedily of; to devour.)*

If William Penn's aunts kept a pastry shop, what would be the current prices of their pies?   *ANS: The pie rates of Penn's aunts (Pirates of Penzance).*

What made the tart tart?   *ANS: She didn't want the baker to bake her.*

Why is a loaf of bread four weeks old like a mouse running into a hole?   *ANS: Because you can see it's stale.*

When may bread be said to be alive?   *ANS: When it has a little Indian in it. ("Indian": Indian corn; maize.)*

What relation is a loaf of bread to a locomotive?   *ANS: The mother. Bread is a necessity, a locomotive is an invention, and "Necessity is the mother of invention."*

Why did the moron go into the street with his bread and butter?   *ANS: He was looking for the traffic jam.*

  Did the moron find the traffic jam?   *ANS: Yes, a truck came along and gave him a big jar.*

Why is a hotcake like a caterpillar?   *ANS: Because it's the grub that makes the butter-fly.*

If a Uneeda Biscuit is a soda cracker, what is an icepick? *ANS: A water cracker.*

Why did the jelly roll?   *ANS: It saw the apple turnover.*

Meat, Fish, Eggs, and Cheese

Why is a chicken pie like a gunsmith's shop?   *ANS: Because it contains fowl-in-pieces.*

Why can you not make a venison pasty of buck venison? *ANS: Because a pasty must be made of dough.*

Why ought meat to be only half cooked?   *ANS: Because what is done cannot be helped.*

Why is a man lifting a side of bacon off a hook to be pitied? *ANS: Because he's a pork-reacher (poor creature).*

How can you buy eggs and be sure they have no chickens in them?   *ANS: Buy duck eggs.*

Why is a promise like an egg? *ANS: Because it is so easily broken.*

> I can throw an egg against the wall,
> And it will neither break nor fall.

ANS: The wall will neither break nor fall.

How many soft-boiled eggs can one eat on an empty stomach? *ANS: Only one; after that the stomach will not be empty.*

Why, in France, is one egg sufficient for a meal?   *ANS: Because an egg is "un oeuf"; and enough is as good as a feast.*

A farmer ate two eggs every morning for his breakfast. He had no chickens; nobody ever gave him any eggs, and he never bought, borrowed, begged, or stole any eggs. Where did he get the eggs?   *ANS: They were duck eggs.*

If cheese comes after dinner, what comes after cheese? *ANS: A mouse.*

What most resembles the half of a cheese?   *ANS: The other half.*

Which is better, complete happiness or a cheese sandwich? *ANS: A cheese sandwich; nothing is better than complete happiness, and a cheese sandwich is better than nothing.*

Other Named Foods

When is sugar like a pig's tooth?   *ANS: When it is in a hogshead.*

Why did the little moron take sugar and cream with him to the movie? *ANS: He heard there was going to be a serial.*

When is soup most likely to run out of the bowl? *ANS: When there is a leek in it.*

What kind of jam cannot be eaten? *ANS: A traffic jam.*

What did the candy bar say to the lollipop? *ANS: "Hello, sucker."*

Why can we never buy salt? *ANS: Salt is for the cellar.*

Where does all the pepper go? *ANS: No one nose.*

What did the mayonnaise say to the refrigerator? *ANS: "Please close the door; I'm dressing."*

Food Workers

Why is a baker a most improvident man? *ANS: Because he is continually selling what he kneads himself.*

Why is a drugstore like a bakery? *ANS: Because it sells pizen things.*

When does a cook not prepare a square meal? *ANS: When she wants it to go round.*

Why is the French cook at the Union Club like a man sitting on the top of a shot tower? *ANS: Because he is in a high culinary (cool and airy) situation.*

Why do fishermen possess such extraordinary medical powers? *ANS: Because they cure dead fish.*

Why can you not expect a fishmonger to be generous? *ANS: Because his business makes him sell-fish.*

Why does the butcher's wife always keep the books? *ANS: Because the business is a joint affair.*

Why is a dealer in sugar and coffee worse than a smuggler? *ANS: Because, while the latter is a gross character, the former is a grocer.*

Why is a baker like a beggar?   *ANS: Because he kneads bread.*

Why are fishermen and shepherds not to be trusted?   *ANS: Because they live by hook and by crook.*

If a waiter were carrying a turkey on a platter and let it fall, what three great national calamities would occur?   *ANS: The downfall of turkey, the breaking up of china, and the overthrow of grease.*

Why is a cook to a king like a bucketful of coal?   *ANS: Because he feeds the great.*

DRINK AND DRINKERS

Appropriate Beverage

What beverage is appropriate for a cowboy?   *ANS: Brandy.*

What beverage is appropriate for a fat man?   *ANS: Stout.*

What beverage is appropriate for a floorwalker?   *ANS: Cordial.*

What beverage is appropriate for a golfer?   *ANS: Tea.*

What beverage is appropriate for a hypochondriac?   *ANS: Champagne.*

What beverage is appropriate for an invalid?   *ANS: Ale.*

What beverage is appropriate for a poultry farmer?   *ANS: Cocktail.*

What beverage is appropriate for a prize fighter?   *ANS: Punch.*

What beverage is appropriate for a sailor?   *ANS: Port.*

What beverage is appropriate for a shoemaker?   *ANS:* *Cobbler.*

What beverage is appropriate for a stock promoter?   *ANS:* Water.

What beverage is appropriate for an undertaker?   *ANS:* *Beer.*

Soft Drinks

Why is this country like milk?   *ANS: Because it's ours.*

When is it socially correct to serve milk in a saucer?   *ANS: When you're feeding the cat.*

With which hand should you stir your cocoa?   *ANS: With either, but it is better to stir it with a spoon.*

Why was the little drop of cider crying?   *ANS: Because all his friends were in the jug.*

Why should a poor man drink coffee?   *ANS: Because he has no proper-ty.*

Why is coffee like a dull knife?   *ANS: Because it has to be ground before it can be used.*

What beverage represents what the patient has and what the doctor gets?   *ANS: Cof-fee.*

What beverage represents the beginning of time?   *ANS: Tea. (T).*

Why is my cup of tea stronger than yours?   *ANS: Because it's all my tea.*

When a man complains because his coffee is cold, what does his wife do?   *ANS: She makes it hot for him.*

Why is fresh milk like something that never happened?   *ANS: Because it hasn't a curd.*

Hard Drink and Drinkers

Why are too much whiskey and brandy like the flowers that bloom in the spring?   *ANS: Because they make the nose gay.*

Why are there three objections to taking a glass of brandy? *ANS: Because there are three scruples to a dram.*

Why is an interesting book like a drunkard's nose?   *ANS: Because it is read to the end.*

Why is a drunkard hesitating to sign the pledge like a skeptical Hindu?   *ANS: Because he is in doubt whether to give up his jug or not.*

Why are heavy drinkers like heavy showers?   *ANS: Because they usually begin with little drops.*

Why is the owner of a wine cellar a person of great self-control?   *ANS: Because, however fiery his spirits may be, he always keeps them in a basement.*

What kind of anchor does a drunken sailor like best?   *ANS: An anker (anchor) of brandy. ("Anker": A liquid measure; in the United States, 10 gallons.*

What man must have his glass before he starts to work? *ANS: A glazier.*

What is the difference between a glass of water and a glass of whiskey?   *ANS: About seventy-five cents.*

6

Earth and Sky

GEOGRAPHY

Europe

Why should England have been so very dry at the beginning of the twentieth century? *ANS: Because there had been only one reign there in more than sixty years.*

What part of London is in France? *ANS: The letter N.*

What extraordinary kind of meat is to be bought in the Isle of Wight? *ANS: Mutton from Cowes.*

Why is a tourist in Ireland like a donkey? *ANS: Because he is going to Bray.*

Why should yellow peas be sent to Hammersmith? *ANS: Because that is the way to Turnham Green.*

Why are horses little needed in the Isle of Wight? *ANS: Because visitors prefer Cowes to Ryde.*

Why may we well doubt the existence of the Blarney Stone? *ANS: Because there are so many shamrocks in Ireland.*

Why should we not believe one word that comes from Holland? *ANS: Because Holland is such a low-lying country.*

Why doesn't Sweden export cattle? *ANS: Because she wants to keep her Stockholm.*

Why is the map of Europe like a frying pan? *ANS: Because it has Greece on the bottom.*

Why is the leaning tower of Pisa like Greenland?   *ANS: Because it is oblique.*

What makes the Tower of Pisa lean?   *ANS: It never eats.*

If a thin man were to dress himself in the clothes of a tall, fat man, what two cities of France would he resemble? *ANS: Toulon and Toulouse.*

Why need France never fear an inundation?   *ANS: Because there the water is always "l'eau."*

Why should you not swim in the river at Paris?   *ANS: Because if you did you would be in Seine.*

Why is Berlin the most dissipated city of Europe?   *ANS: Because it is always on the Spree.*

United States

What is the happiest state in the union?   *ANS: Merry land.*

What did Tennessee?   *ANS: Exactly what Arkansas.*

What else did Tennessee?   *ANS: It saw Ida-ho.*

If Miss Issippi should lend Miss Ouri her New Jersey, what would Dela-ware?   *ANS: I don't know, but Alaska.*

Why is a man hurrying to prevent his daughter Hannah falling over a precipice like one journeying to a city in the South?   *ANS: Because he is going to save Hannah.*

Why should one not gaze at Niagara Falls too long?   *ANS: Because he might get a cataract in his eye.*

How do sailors identify Long Island?   *ANS: By the sound.*

What would you do if you found Chicago, Ill.?   *ANS: Call a Baltimore M-d.*

What is the highest public building in Boston?   *ANS: The public library has the most stories.*

What state produces the most marriages? *ANS: The state of matrimony.*

Which state is round at both ends and high in the middle? *ANS: O-hi-o.*

What part of New York is in Chicago? *ANS: The letter O.*

What is found in the middle of both America and Australia? *ANS: The letter R.*

Other Named Places

Why is Canada like courtship? *ANS: Because it borders on the United States.*

If you were to throw a white stone into the Red Sea, what would it become? *ANS: Wet.*

Why do so many Chinese travel on foot? *ANS: Because there is only one Cochin China.*

Why is a pleasure trip to Egypt fit only for very old gentlemen? *ANS: Because it is a see-Nile thing to do.*

If a man is born in Turkey, grows up in Italy, comes to America, and dies in Chicago, what is he? *ANS: Dead.*

Is there much difference between the North Pole and the South Pole? *ANS: Yes, all the difference in the world.*

What Place?

What is the most warlike nation? *ANS: Vaccination, for it is almost always in arms.*

What country ought to be the richest in the world? *ANS: Ireland, for its capital is always Dublin.*

What country makes you shiver? *ANS: Chile.*

What country is like a happy dog? *ANS: A-merry-cur.*

With the name of a country, tell what the mother asked her crying child.   *ANS: Are you Hungary?*

What did the child reply?   *ANS: Yes, Siam.*

What did the mother say next?   *ANS: Come along, then, I'll Fiji.*

What did she give him to eat?   *ANS: A slice of Turkey.*

Why did the child start crying again?   *ANS: He wanted Samoa.*

What did the mother say that time?   *ANS: Stop those Wales.*

What island is six-sided?   *ANS: Cuba.*

What islands are the most social?   *ANS: The Society Islands.*

In what island would an easy-going bachelor choose to live? *ANS: In Ceylon, because he would be sure of finding Singhalese there.*

What was the largest island before Australia was discovered? *ANS: Australia.*

What islands would form a cheerful luncheon party?   *ANS: Friendly, Society, Sandwich, and Madeira.*

What sea is most traveled by clever people?   *ANS: Brillian-cy.*

In what sea would a man most like to be on a wet day? *ANS: A-dri-atic.*

Which is the coldest river?   *ANS: The Isis.*

What river is ever without a beginning and ending?   *ANS: Severn; S-ever-N.*

What river in Austria answers the question, "Who is there?" *ANS: Iser.*

What is the most difficult river on which to get a boat?
ANS: The Arno, because they're Arno boats there.

What river runs between two seas?   *ANS: The Thames,
which runs between Battersea and Chelsea.*

HEAVENLY BODIES

What holds the moon up?   *ANS: The moon-beams.*

Upon what does the moon have more effect than on the tide?
ANS: Upon the untied.

When is the moon like a load of hay?   *ANS: When it is
on the wane. ("Wain": A four-wheeled vehicle for the trans-
portation of goods, produce, etc.)*

Why can the world never come to an end?   *ANS: Because
it is round.*

Why is the sun like a man about town?   *ANS: Because it
turns night into day.*

If I were in the sun and U (you) were out of the sun, what
would the sun become?   *ANS: Sin.*

Why are fixed stars like wicked old men?   *ANS: Because
they scin-til-late.*

What constellation resembles an empty fireplace?   *ANS:
The Great Bear.*

Why are a star and an old barn alike?   *ANS: Because
both contain r-a-t-s.*

WATER, WIND, AND WEATHER

Why doesn't the ocean overflow the land?   *ANS: Because
it's tide.*

When will water stop running downhill?   *ANS: When
it reaches the bottom.*

When can you carry water in a sieve?   *ANS: When it is frozen.*

When does water resemble a gymnast?   *ANS: When it makes a spring.*

What does a stone become when it falls into the water? *ANS: A wet stone (whetstone).*

When a boy falls into the water, what is the first thing that he does?   *ANS: Get wet.*

What makes the waves so wild?   *ANS: Having the wind blow them up. ("Blow up": To scold or abuse violently.)*

What sort of wind do we look for after Lent?   *ANS: An Easter-ly one.*

Why does the north wind in winter not blow straight? *ANS: Because it blows so bleak.*

Prove that the wind is blind.   *ANS: The wind is a breeze; a breeze is a zephyr; a zephyr is a yarn; a yarn is a tale; a tail is an appendage; an appendage is an attachment; an attachment is love; and love is blind.*

Why does the air seem fresher in winter than it does in summer?   *ANS: Because it is kept on ice most of the time.*

Which moves faster, heat or cold?   *ANS: Heat, for you can catch cold.*

When you look around on a cold winter day, what do you see on every hand?   *ANS: A glove.*

When is the weather worst for rats and mice?   *ANS: When it rains cats and dogs.*

When is the weather best for haymaking?   *ANS: When it rains pitchforks.*

What heavenly thing, and what earthly thing, does a rainy day most affect?   *ANS: The sun and your shoes; it takes the shine from both.*

When does the rain become too familiar with a young lady? *ANS: When it begins to patter on her back.*

What always happens at the end of a dry spell?   *ANS: It rains.*

Why is a cloud like Santa Claus?   *ANS: Because it holds the rain, dear.*

When is a man like frozen rain?   *ANS: When he is hale.*

Instead of complaining when it rains, we should do as they do in Spain. What is that?   *ANS: Let it rain.*

What is worse than raining cats and dogs?   *ANS: Hailing taxicabs.*

Why is a warm day bad for an icicle's character?   *ANS: Because it turns it into an eavesdropper.*

Why is a heavy fall of snow easily understood?   *ANS: Because one can see the drift.*

Why is snow different from Sunday?   *ANS: Because it can fall on any day of the week.*

7

History, Government, and Law

HISTORY

Where did Caesar go on his thirty-ninth birthday? *ANS: Into his fortieth year.*

Why is Athens like a worn-out shoe? *ANS: Because it once had a Solon.*

Why are the Middle Ages called the Dark Ages? *ANS: Because there were so many knights then.*

Captain Cook made three voyages around the world and was killed on one of these voyages. On which one? *ANS: The last one.*

Why were Queen Victoria's poultry quarrelsome? *ANS: Because they were Vic's hens.*

What English king had a naturally great aversion to washerwomen? *ANS: John, because of his great losses in the Wash.*

What celebrated man in history might you name if you wished your servant to replenish your fire? *ANS: Philip the Great.*

Why was Lord Nelson like a coward? *ANS: Because the last thing Nelson did was to die for his country, and that's about the last thing a coward will do.*

What was it that Queen Mary had before and King William had behind and Queen Anne didn't have at all? *ANS: The letter M.*

Why could Napoleon III not insure his life? *ANS: Because no man living could make out his policy.*

Why would you prefer the death of Joan of Arc to that of Mary, Queen of Scots? *ANS: Because a hot steak is preferable to a cold chop.*

Can you tell me of what parentage Napoleon I was? *ANS: Of Corsican.*

Why was a medieval tournament like sleep? *ANS: Because it was a knightly occupation.*

Why was Columbus a very dissipated man? *ANS: Because he has been on a bust for four hundred years.*

Why is an owl in the daylight like a former President of the United States? *ANS: Because he's a-blinkin'.*

What did the Pilgrims do when they landed in this country? *ANS: First they fell on their knees, and then they fell on the aborigines.*

What did Paul Revere say when he finished his famous ride? *ANS: "Whoa."*

In what way are most of us like Columbus? *ANS: He did not know where he was going when he started; he did not know where he was when he got there; and he did not know where he had been when he got back.*

Why was Washington buried at Mt. Vernon? *ANS: Because he was dead.*

What girl did the most damage in the Civil War? *ANS: Minnie Ball. ("Minié ball": After the inventor, Captain C. E. Minié, of France—a kind of conical rifle bullet, much used in the middle of the nineteenth century.)*

ROYALTY AND NOBILITY

Where are kings usually crowned? *ANS: On the head.*

What is Majesty deprived of its externals?   *ANS: A jest (m-a jest-y).*

Who dares to sit before the Queen with his hat on?   *ANS: Her coachman.*

Why is Buckingham Palace the cheapeast palace ever built? *ANS: Because it was built for one sovereign and furnished for another.*

When are two kings like three miles?   *ANS: When they make a league.*

Why is it wise for a king to have several court jesters? *ANS: Because in that way he always keeps his wits about him.*

There has been but one king crowned in England since the Conquest. What king was he?   *ANS: James I. He was King of Scotland before he was King of England. The others were not kings until after they were crowned.*

Why is the Prince of Wales like a cloudy day?   *ANS: Because he is likely to reign.*

Why does a nobleman's title sometimes become extinct? *ANS: Because, though the king can make a man a peer (appear), he cannot make him a parent.*

GOVERNMENT AND POLITICS

Why is a vote in Congress like a bad cold?   *ANS: Because sometimes the ayes have it, and sometimes the noes.*

What is the difference between Congress and progress? *ANS: Pro and con.*

Why are many politicians like lobsters?   *ANS: Because they change color when they get into hot water.*

Why is a mouse entering a mousetrap like a diplomat arguing his policy?   *ANS: Because he has a well-defined end in view.*

Why is a man who gets knocked down at an election like the world that we inhabit?   *ANS: Because he is flattened at the polls.*

Why are British parliamentary reports called Blue Books? *ANS: Because they are never read.*

What Tory do the Whigs want on their side?   *ANS: Victory.*

Why is a member of Parliament like a shrimp?   *ANS: Because he has M. P. at the end of his name.*

LAWYERS AND LAWCOURTS

Why is a young lawyer in his office like one of his chickens roosting on his neighbor's fence?   *ANS: Because he has no business there.*

Why is a competent lawyer like a bloodstone set in jet? *ANS: Because he is deep read in Blackstone.*

What is a lawyer's favorite pudding?   *ANS: Sue-it.*

Why is a lawyer like a clergyman?   *ANS: Because he studies the law, and profits.*

When is a lawyer like a donkey?   *ANS: When he draws a conveyance.*

Why is a lawyer like a crow?   *ANS: Because he likes to have his cause heard.*

When is a lawyer like circumstances?   *ANS: When he alters cases.*

What proverb must a lawyer not follow?   *ANS: He must not take the will for the deed.*

Why is an ignorant lawyer like necessity?   *ANS: Because he knows no law.*

Why is a judge's nose like the middle of the earth?   *ANS: Because it is the center of gravity.*

Why cannot a deaf man be legally convicted?   *ANS: Because it is unlawful to condemn a man without a hearing.*

Why is a prisoner on trial like a criminal hanging?   *ANS: Because he's in a state of suspense.*

COPS AND ROBBERS

Why are policemen like the days of man?   *ANS: Because they are numbered.*

Why is electricity like the police when they are wanted? *ANS: Because it is an invisible force.*

Why is a burglar upstairs an honest man?   *ANS: Because he is above doing something dishonest.*

Why is a professional thief comfortable?   *ANS: Because he takes things easy.*

What is the least dangerous kind of robbery?   *ANS: Safe robbery.*

Why is a thief like a tired man?   *ANS: Because he needs arresting.*

Why can a thief be said to be broadminded?   *ANS: Because he is open to conviction.*

Why is a thief called a jailbird?   *ANS: Because he has been a-robbin'.*

In what room of the house that he robs is a burglar most likely to be interested?   *ANS: In the haul.*

Why are criminals like bachelors?   *ANS: Because they don't like to go to court.*

Why do handcuffs resemble suitcases?   *ANS: Because they are made for two wrists.*

Why is a man in jail like a boat full of water?   *ANS: Because he requires bailing out.*

Why is the window of a jail like a nutmeg?   *ANS: Because it has to be grated to be useful.*

Why is a treadmill run by convicts like a true convert? *ANS: Because its turning is the result of conviction.*

Why is a man committing murder like a hen walking across the street?   *ANS: Because it's a foul (fowl) proceeding.*

What is the most dangerous kind of assassin?   *ANS: One who takes life cheerfully.*

Why is the gallows the last refuge of a condemned man? *ANS: He has nothing else to depend upon.*

8

Home, Church, and School

HOME

House, Yard, and Farm

Why is a dilapidated house like a very old man? *ANS: Because its gate is feeble and its locks are few.*

Why is the house of a tidy wife like a motion to adjourn? *ANS: Because it is always in order.*

What is all over the house? *ANS: The roof.*

Why did the moron sit on top of the house? *ANS: He had heard that the treats were on the house.*

A man came home without his key and found all the doors and windows locked. How did he get in? *ANS: He raced around the house until he was "all in."*

What is the surest way to keep water from coming into your house? *ANS: Don't pay your water bill.*

What affections do landlords most appreciate? *ANS: Pay-rental.*

What runs all around the yard without moving? *ANS: The fence.*

What had better be done when there is a great rent on the farm? *ANS: It had better be sown.*

What is the greatest eyesore in a farmyard? *ANS: A pig-sty.*

What is the largest room in the world?   *ANS: Room for improvement.*

If a man bumped his head against the top of the room, what article of stationery would he be supplied with?   *ANS: Ceiling whacks.*

What did the chimney and the door do when the house caught on fire?   *ANS: The chimney flue and the door bolted.*

What did one wall say to the other wall?   *ANS: "I'll meet you at the corner."*

What did the rug say to the floor?   *ANS: "Hands up; I've got you covered."*

What relation is a door-mat to a door-step?   *ANS: A step-fa'ther.*

When is a door not a door?   *ANS: When it's ajar.*

Why is a lock like a hospital?   *ANS: Because it has wards in it.*

When should a window pane blush?   *ANS: When it sees the weather-strip.*

How does the fireplace feel when you fill it with coal? *ANS: Grate-full.*

What will go up the chimney down and down the chimney down, but will not go up the chimney up nor down the chimney up?   *ANS: An umbrella.*

Why must chimney sweeping be a very agreeable business? *ANS: Because it soots everyone who tries it.*

Furniture, Equipment, and Utensils

When does a chair dislike you?   *ANS: When it can't bear you.*

When is a chair like a woman's dress?   *ANS: When it is sat-in.*

Why is an old chair with a new bottom like a paid bill? *ANS: Because it has been re-seated.*

Why did the moron sleep on the chandelier?   *ANS: Because he was a light sleeper.*

Why is an uncomfortable chair like comfort?   *ANS: Because it is devoid of ease (E's).*

Why is a sleepy person like a carpet?   *ANS: Because he will have his nap.*

What is the most striking thing in the way of a mantel ornament?   *ANS: A clock.*

Why is a mirror like a resolution?   *ANS: Because it is so easily broken.*

When you move from one house to another, why should you not take the washbasins with you?   *ANS: Because they are not ewers.*

How many sides has a pitcher?   *ANS: Two; outside and inside.*

Domestic Supplies and Activities

Why has a chambermaid more lives than a cat?   *ANS: Because each morning she returns to dust.*

Why is a butler like a mountain?   *ANS: Because he looks down on the valet.*

What is the hardest soap?   *ANS: Castile.*

What is the best way to remove paint?   *ANS: Sit down on it before it is dry.*

What goes most against a farmer's grain?   *ANS: His reaper.*

Which burns longer, a wax candle or a tallow candle? *ANS: Neither; they both burn shorter.*

If you woke up in the night, what would you do for a light? *ANS: Take a feather from the pillow; that's light enough.*

What happens to a lighted match when you drop it into a river?   *ANS: It goes out.*

Why is an empty matchbox superior to all other boxes? *ANS: Because it is matchless.*

When is a candle like an ill-conditioned, quarrelsome man? *ANS: When it is put out before it has had time to flare up and blaze away.*

CHURCH, CLERGYMEN, AND RELIGION

Why does a hen never preach?   *ANS: Because she belongs to the lay element.*

Why does a preacher have an easier time than a doctor or a lawyer?   *ANS: Because it is easier to preach than to practice.*

Why does the average preacher need no umbrella when going to his church on a rainy day?   *ANS: Because he is sure to be dry when he gets into the pulpit.*

Why can no clergyman have a wooden leg?   *ANS: Because, although a chaplain may be a plain chap, a parson cannot be a layman (lame 'un).*

Why is a clergyman of the Church of England the most untrustworthy of preachers?   *ANS: Because he is never long a curate (accurate) if he can help it.*

Why is a theological student like a chicken served to a preacher?   *ANS: Because he is about to enter the ministry.*

Why are many sermons like asparagus?   *ANS: Because it is the ends of them that people enjoy most.*

Why should free seats at church be abolished?   *ANS: Because they make people good for nothing.*

Why is Westminster Abbey like a fireplace?   *ANS: Because it contains the ashes of the great.*

What gates are like church bells?   *ANS: Toll gates.*

Why are church bells the most obedient of inanimate objects?   *ANS: Because they make a noise whenever they are tolled.*

On which side of a country church is the graveyard always situated?   *ANS: The outside.*

If the Devil were to lose his tail, where should he go to get another?   *ANS: To a liquor store, where bad spirits are retailed.*

Why is the Devil always a gentleman?   *ANS: Because, being the imp o' darkness, he can never be imp o' light.*

Why are umbrellas like good churchmen?   *ANS: Because they keep lent so well.*

How many wives does the English prayer book allow a man to have?   *ANS: Sixteen; for better, for worse, for richer, for poorer.*

If a woman were to change her sex, why could she no longer be a Christian?   *ANS: Because she would be a he then.*

What kind of men are very apt to worship their maker?
ANS: Self-made men.

What is Holy Water?   *ANS: Ordinary water with the Hell boiled out of it.*

What kind of men go to Heaven?   *ANS: Dead men.*

> What's in the church, but not the steeple?
> The parson has it, but not the people.

ANS: The letter R.

What changes the lower regions into the flower regions?
ANS: The letter F.

SCHOOL, TEACHERS, AND STUDENTS

Why is a schoolboy being flogged like your eye?   *ANS: Because he is a pupil under the lash.*

Why is a good speller in a spelling bee like a glass of champagne?   *ANS: Because he goes to the head.*

When is a schoolboy like a postage stamp?   *ANS: When he is licked and put in the corner to make him stick to his letters.*

What insect frequents district schools?   *ANS: The spelling bee.*

Why are schoolmasters and their pupils like dogs and cats? *ANS: Because one is of the canin', the other of the feelin', species.*

Why did Johnny's teacher put him in the B class?   *ANS: Because he had hives.*

On the desk of a certain country schoolteacher is a bell which she uses for signaling class periods. You've been told the teacher's name. What is it?   *ANS: Isabel.*

Why is a college freshman like a telescope?   *ANS: Because he is easily drawn out, seen through, and shut up.*

Why is education like a tailor?   *ANS: Because it forms our habits.*

Why does a student never lead a sedentary life?   *ANS: Because he's always pursuing his studies.*

Why is a woman, when blindfolded, like an ignorant schoolteacher?   *ANS: Because her pupils are kept in the dark.*

How many books can a student put into an empty schoolbag?   *ANS: One; after that the bag will not be empty.*

When is a rope like a child at school?   *ANS: When it is taut.*

9

Literature and Language;
Speech and Writing

AUTHORS

How do we know that Lord Byron was good-tempered? *ANS: Because he always kept his collar down.*

How do we know that Byron did not wear a wig? *ANS: Because everybody admired his Corsair so much.*

What proof have we that Cowper was in debt? *ANS: He "oh'd" for a lodge in some vast wilderness.*

Why is it almost certain that Shakespeare was a broker? *ANS: Because he has furnished more stock quotations than any other man.*

Who wrote the most—Dickens, Warren, or Bulwer? *ANS: Dickens. Warren wrote "Now and Then," Bulwer wrote "Night and Morning," but Dickens wrote "All the Year Round."*

When is a pie like a poet? *ANS: When it is browning.*

Why are people who write books so funny looking? *ANS: Because their tales come right out of their heads.*

What is the most puzzling thing an author can write about? *ANS: A piece of string, because it has two different ends.*

Why is a blundering writer like an arbiter in a dispute? *ANS: Because he writes wrong.*

What English poet does a mummy resemble? *ANS: Dried 'un.*

What author would eyeglasses mention to the world if they could only speak?   *ANS: You-see-by-us.*

What author: "Thousands by me have met their death; all nature withers at my breath"?   *ANS: Frost.*

What author: "Each living head in time, 'tis said, will turn to him though he be dead"?   *ANS: Gray.*

If a tough beefsteak could talk, what English poet would it mention?   *ANS: Chaw, sir.*

"Mamma is in perfect health, my child," and thus he named a poet mild.   *ANS: Motherwell.*

What American author may be considered equal to three-fifths of all the poets ancient and modern?   *ANS: Poe.*

If you saw a house on fire, what three poets' names might you pronounce?   *ANS: Dickens, Howitt Burns.*

BOOKS IN GENERAL; PERIODICALS

Why are the pages of a book like the days of man?   *ANS: Because they are numbered.*

When is an apple like a book?   *ANS: When it is red.*

What is the difference between a book and a bore?   *ANS: You can shut up a book.*

When is a book like a prisoner in the states of Barbary?   *ANS: When it is bound in morocco.*

When is a newspaper like a delicate child?   *ANS: When it is weekly.*

Why should "Watermelon" be a good name for a newspaper?   *ANS: Because its insides would be sure to be red.*

SPECIFIC WRITINGS

Who in all of Shakespeare's plays killed the greatest number of ducks and chickens?   *ANS: Hamlet's uncle, because he "did murder most foul."*

Why is the letter R like the face of Hamlet's father? *ANS: Because it is "more in sorrow than in anger."*

Why should a favorite hen be called "Macduff"?   *ANS: Because we wish her to lay on.*

Why cannot the Irish properly perform the play *Hamlet*? *ANS: Because they cannot help making "Aphalia" of the heroine.*

What reason is there to believe that Othello was a lawyer? *ANS: He was a tawny general of Venice.*

Why is a pig with a curly tail like the ghost of Hamlet's father?   *ANS: Because he could a tail unfold.*

If Falstaff had been musical, what instrument would he have chosen after dinner?   *ANS: The sackbut. ("Sackbut": An early form of the slide trombone; a butt, or cask, of sack, which is a kind of wine.)*

Why was *Uncle Tom's Cabin* not written by a female hand? *ANS: Because it was written by Harriet Beecher Stowe (Beecher's toe).*

What best describes and impedes a pilgrim's progress? *ANS: Bunyan.*

Why is it a mistake to believe that Robinson Crusoe's island was uninhabited?   *ANS: Because the very first thing that Crusoe saw on landing was a great swell pitching into a little cove on the shore.*

Why is this book like giving you your choice of two kinds of meat for dinner?   *ANS: Because it is before you (beef or ewe).*

Why is a carrot like this book?   *ANS: Because it can't be beet.*

LEGEND AND MYTH

Why is a coach going downhill like St. George?   *ANS: Because it is always drawn with the drag-on.*

Why are temperance hotels like the Elysium of the gods? *ANS: Because no bad spirits are allowed to enter them.*

If Britannia were deformed, what English public institution would she remind you of?   *ANS: The National Gal-awry.*

Why does Santa Claus always go down the chimney?   *ANS: Because it soots him.*

Why is a Greek fable like a garret?   *ANS: Because it is an Attic story.*

Why is Orpheus always in bad company?   *ANS: Because you never see him without a lyre.*

How did Little Bo-peep lose her sheep?   *ANS: She had a crook with her.*

LANGUAGE AND GRAMMAR

What grammatical term is most distasteful to lovers?   *ANS: The third person.*

Do you say, "Nine and five *are* thirteen" or "Nine and five *is* thirteen"?   *ANS: Neither, for nine and five are fourteen.*

What is the superlative of *temper*?   *ANS: Tempest.*

What are the three degrees of getting on in the world? *ANS: Get on, get honor, get honest.*

Why is the word GIRL not a noun?   *ANS: Because ALAS is an interjection.*

How do you parse the word KISS?   *ANS: Noun, proper, plural, although singular if I should decline it; also a conjunction, and it agrees with me.*

Which is better: "The house burned *down*" or "The house burned up"?   *ANS: Neither; they are both very bad.*

How do eggs show their anger on being called "heggs"? *ANS: By becoming eggs aspirated.*

In what sort of syllables ought a parrot to speak?   *ANS: In polly-syllables.*

How would you punctuate this sentence: "I saw a five-dollar bill on the street"?   *ANS: I would make a dash after it.*

What language does an Arabian child speak before it cuts its teeth?   *ANS: Gum Arabic.*

Why is a door always in the subjunctive mood?   *ANS: Because it is always wood, or should be.*

SPEECH AND HANDWRITING

Secrets

Why is whispering prohibited in company?   *ANS: Because it is not aloud.*

What can you break with a whisper more easily than with a hammer?   *ANS: A secret.*

What burns to keep a secret?   *ANS: Sealing wax.*

In what color should a secret be kept?   *ANS: Inviolate.*

Questions

Why is our last question like a young lady sitting on a pile of theological books?   *ANS: Because it is vergin' on something serious.*

What asks no questions, but receives lots of answers? *ANS: A telephone.*

Ask a question that must be answered "Yes." *ANS: "What does Y-E-S spell?"*

Ask a question that cannot be answered "Yes." *ANS: "Are you asleep?"*

Why is a person who asks questions the strangest of all individuals? *ANS: Because he is the querist.*

Truth and Falsehood

How can a man tell the naked truth? *ANS: By giving the bare facts.*

Why is a lie like a wig? *ANS: Because it is a false-hood.*

How can you always find a liar out? *ANS: By going to his house when he isn't in.*

When is a man obliged to keep his word? *ANS: When no one else will take it.*

Gossip and Loquacity

Why should one not gossip in a wheatfield? *ANS: Because he might shock the wheat.*

Why is a busybody like tallow? *ANS: Because he makes scandals.*

Why is a piece of gossip like a cigarette? *ANS: Because it is in every idler's mouth.*

What makes the best eavesdropper? *ANS: An icicle.*

Why are tedious talkers like very old people? *ANS: Because they dilate.*

Why is a talkative young man like a young pig? *ANS: Because if he lives he is likely to become a great bore.*

Other Kinds of Talk

Why is it impossible for a man who lisps to believe in the existence of young ladies?   *ANS: Because to him every miss is a "mith."*

Why should you never tell a man to take a back seat? *ANS: Because if you do he is likely to take affront.*

What constitutes a weighty discourse?   *ANS: First to announce a text, and then to ex-pound it.*

Why is a lecture on board ship like a young lady's necklace? *ANS: Because it is a deck-oration.*

Handwriting

What kind of pen does a plagiarist use?   *ANS: Steal.*

When is longhand quicker than shorthand?   *ANS: When it is on a clock.*

Why is a man who makes pens a wicked man?   *ANS: Because he makes men steel pens, and then says they do write.*

Why is a lead pencil like a perverse child?   *ANS: Because it never does write by itself.*

10

Women; Love, Courtship, and Marriage

WOMEN

Why is a pretty girl like an excellent mirror?   *ANS: Because she is a good looking lass.*

Why are a beautiful fascinating young lady and a butcher alike?   *ANS: Because they are both killing creatures.*

Why is a bright and pretty young lady like a spoon in a cup of tea?   *ANS: Because she is in-tea-resting.*

Why is an attractive young woman like a successful gambler?   *ANS: Because she has such winning ways.*

Why is a pretty woman like a hinge?   *ANS: Because she is something to adore.*

Who are the largest two ladies in the United States?   *ANS: Miss Ouri and Mrs. Sippi.*

Why is it impossible for a pretty girl to be candid?   *ANS: Because she cannot be plain.*

What is more moist than a young lady with waves in her hair, a cataract in her eye, and a crick in her back?   *ANS: One with a notion in her head.*

Where is it that all women are equally beautiful?   *ANS: In the dark.*

What is the difference between a woman and an umbrella?   *ANS: You can shut an umbrella up.*

73

When is a woman deformed?   *ANS: When mending stockings, because she then has her hands where her feet ought to be.*

Why can you never tell a woman's real hysterics from her sham ones?   *ANS: Because in either case it's a faint (feint).*

Why are good intentions like fainting women?   *ANS: Because all they need is carrying out.*

Why is a woman like an angel?   *ANS: Because she's usually up in the air, she's always harping on something, and she never has anything to wear.*

Why are some women like facts?   *ANS: Because they are stubborn things.*

Why is a melancholy young lady like the most entertaining of companions?   *ANS: Because she is always a-musing.*

Why is a young woman like an arrow?   *ANS: Because she is in a quiver until she gets a beau, and can't go anywhere without one.*

How many young women would it take to reach from New York to Philadelphia?   *ANS: About one hundred, for a miss is as good as a mile.*

What can a man give to a woman that he can't give to a man? *ANS: His name.*

What does a young woman become when she ceases to be pensive?   *ANS: Ex-pensive.*

What three acts comprise the chief business of a woman's life?   *ANS: Attract, contract, detract.*

When is a maiden most chaste?   *ANS: When she is most run after.*

Why are women like the ocean?   *ANS: Because they never dry up.*

Why is a woman's age like a bell without a clapper? *ANS: Because it is never told.*

Why is a nice but uncultured girl like brown sugar? *ANS: Because she is sweet but unrefined.*

Why are some women much like teakettles? *ANS: Because they sing away pleasantly, and then all at once boil over.*

Why are women like umbrellas? *ANS: Because they are made out of ribs; you have to dress them up in silk to make them look their best; at the least bit of storm they go right up in the air; it is usually your best friend who takes them away from you; and they are accustomed to reign.*

Why are a vain young lady and a confirmed drunkard alike? *ANS: Because neither of them is satisfied with a moderate use of the glass.*

How do young women show their dislike of mustaches? *ANS: By setting their faces against them.*

A woman who works in a candy store in Milwaukee has measurements of 40-26-40. She is 5 feet 4 inches tall and wears a size nine shoe. What do you think she weighs? *ANS: She weighs candy.*

Why can the pallbearers at a young lady's funeral never be thirsty? *ANS: Because they have a gal on a bier between them.*

> There was a girl in our town,
> Silk an' satin was her gown,
> Silk an' satin, gold an' velvet;
> Guess her name, three times I've telled it.

ANS: Anne.

What is the worth of a woman? *ANS: W (double you), O man.*

What is a French woman worth? *ANS: Two French-women equal deux Françaises; deux francs seize equal 2 francs, 16 centimes; therefore, one Frenchwoman is worth 1 franc, 8 centimes.*

LOVE AND LOVERS

How would you measure a lover's sincerity?   *ANS: By his sighs.*

Why is a bashful lover like popcorn?   *ANS: Because he turns white when he pops.*

Why is love like a piece of heavy baggage on a train trip? *ANS: Because if you don't check it you'll have to express it.*

What two beaus can every girl have near at hand?   *ANS: El-bows.*

If thirty-two is the freezing point, what is the squeezing point?   *ANS: Two in the shade.*

Why is love like a canal boat?   *ANS: Because it is an internal transport.*

Why is ardent love like a circus?   *ANS: Because it is intense.*

Why is reciprocated love like gout?   *ANS: Because it is a joint affection.*

When is a man in love like a tailor?   *ANS: When he is pressing his suit.*

Why is Cupid a poor marksman?   *ANS: Because he is always making Mrs.*

What is the best way to start courting?   *ANS: Get a little gal-an'-try.*

Why did the man call his sweetheart "Postscript"?   *ANS: Because her name was Adeline Moore.*

When a young man calls upon his sweetheart, what should he carry with him?   *ANS: Affection in his heart, perfection in his manners, and confections in his pocket.*

Why is falling in love like catching the measles?   *ANS: Because the older you are when it happens, the harder it goes with you.*

What makes a lover jealous? *ANS: The arrival of a rival.*

Why should one never make love in a vegetable garden? *ANS: Because the potatoes have eyes, the corn has ears, and the beanstalk.*

Why should a broken-hearted young male lodger offer his heart in payment to his landlady? *ANS: Because it is rent.*

Why is absence like a pair of bellows? *ANS: Because it strengthens a strong flame and extinguishes a weak one.*

Why is a lover's heart like a whale? *ANS: Because it's a secreter of great sighs (sea creature of great size).*

Why does a woman like to squeeze her lover? *ANS: Because it makes him flatter.*

What antique weapon does an angry lover represent? *ANS: A cross-bow.*

Why is a lover like a door knocker? *ANS: Because he is bound to adore.*

What did the girl say to her boy friend when he threatened to jump off a cliff? *ANS: "That's a lot of bluff."*

PROPOSALS, ENGAGEMENTS, AND WEDDINGS

Why is a marriage proposal like the first conviction for drunkenness? *ANS: Because it is a short sentence that generally leads to a long one.*

How does Patrick propose to get over his single blessedness? *ANS: By proposing to Bridget.*

When a fast young man says, "I think I had better marry and settle down," what would you advise him instead? *ANS: "Better stay single and settle up."*

Why is a young man engaged to a girl like a man sailing for a port in France?   *ANS: Because he is bound to have-her.*

Why should a bachelor never marry a girl named Ann? *ANS: Because AN is always an indefinite article.*

Why cannot the man in the moon get married?   *ANS: Because he gets only a quarter a week, and he needs that to get full on.*

Why is a man who marries twice like the captain of a ship? *ANS: Because he has a second mate.*

Why is a bride always unlucky on her wedding day?   *ANS: Because she does not marry the best man.*

If two San Francisco telegraph operators were married, what would they become?   *ANS: A Western Union.*

> Pray tell me, ladies, if you can,
> Who is that highly favored man,
> Who though he has married many a wife,
> May still be single all his life?

ANS: A clergyman.

KISSES

What is the shape of a kiss?   *ANS: A-lip-tickle.*

Why is a kiss over the telephone like a straw hat?   *ANS: Because it's not felt.*

What is the naval definition of a kiss?   *ANS: A pleasure smack.*

Why do girls kiss each other, and men not?   *ANS: Girls have nothing better to kiss, and men do.*

Why are a girl's kisses like olives in a jar?   *ANS: Because after you get the first one the rest come easy.*

Why are two young ladies kissing each other an emblem of Christianity?   *ANS: Because they are doing unto each other as they would men should do unto them.*

Why is a man climbing a volcano like an Irishman trying to kiss a girl?   *ANS: Because he is trying to get at the crater's mouth.*

When are kisses sweetest?   *ANS: When sirup-titiously obtained.*

Why is a frankfurter in a refrigerator like a kiss?   *ANS: Because it is dog-on-ice.*

MARRIED PEOPLE

Wife's Name

What is the best name for the wife of an astronomer? *ANS: Stella.*

What is the best name for the wife of a bass singer?   *ANS: Aurora.*

What is the best name for the wife of a chemist?   *ANS: Ann Eliza.*

What is the best name for the wife of a civil engineer? *ANS: Bridget.*

What is the best name for the wife of a dancing master? *ANS: Grace.*

What is the best name for the wife of a doctor?   *ANS: Patience.*

What is the best name for the wife of a fisherman?   *ANS: Nettie.*

What is the best name for the wife of a gambler?   *ANS: Betty.*

What is the best name for the wife of a gardener?   *ANS: Flora.*

What is the best name for the wife of a gas man?   *ANS: Meta.*

What is the best name for the wife of a humorist?   *ANS: Sally.*

What is the best name for the wife of a jeweler?   *ANS: Ruby.*

What is the best name for the wife of a judge?   *ANS: Justine.*

What is the best name for the wife of a lawyer?   *ANS: Sue*

What is the best name for the wife of a marksman?   *ANS: Amy.*

What is the best name for the wife of an outlaw?   *ANS: Roberta.*

What is the best name for the wife of a pianist?   *ANS: Octavia.*

What is the best name for the wife of a redcap?   *ANS: Carrie.*

What is the best name for the wife of a pugilist?   *ANS: Mamie.*

What is the best name for the wife of a Pullman conductor?   *ANS: Bertha.*

What is the best name for the wife of a real-estate man?   *ANS: Lottie.*

What is the best name for the wife of a sexton?   *ANS: Belle.*

What is the best name for the wife of a shoemaker?   *ANS: Peggy.*

What is the best name for the wife of an upholsterer?   *ANS: Sophie.*

Husband and Wife

What beats a good wife? *ANS: A bad husband.*

Why does a wife hug her husband? *ANS: Because she wants to get around him.*

What unripe fruit does a newly married couple resemble? *ANS: A green pair.*

Why are two watches given as prizes like a happy married couple? *ANS: Because though they are two, yet they are won.*

What is a well-matched pair? *ANS: A horsy man and a naggy wife.*

Why is a wife like a newspaper? *ANS: Because every man should have one of his own, and not borrow his neighbor's.*

Why does a man permit himself to be henpecked? *ANS: Because he's chicken-hearted.*

When does a woman think her husband is a Hercules? *ANS: When he is fond of his club.*

What kind of medicine does a man take when he has a scolding wife? *ANS: He takes an elixir.*

Why is a man who beats his wife like a thoroughbred horse? *ANS: Because he's a perfect brute.*

Why is a good wife like the Devil? *ANS: Because while the husbandman sleepeth she seweth tears (soweth tares).*

Why should the Devil make a good husband? *ANS: Because the deuce can never be trey.*

Why is a room packed with married people like an empty room? *ANS: Because there is not a single person in it.*

Why are a wife's complainings like a good security for a man? *ANS: Because they are home rails. ("Home rails": London Stock Exchange—shares of domestic railroads.)*

As I was going to St. Ives,
I met a man with seven wives;
Every wife had seven sacks.
Every sack had seven cats.
Every cat had seven kits.
Kits, cats, sacks, and wives,
How many were going to St. Ives?
ANS: One; the rest came from there.

SINGLE PEOPLE

Why are bachelors like old wood?   *ANS: Because it is hard to get them started, but when they do take flame they burn prodigiously.*

Why does a spinster wear cotton gloves?   *ANS: Because she hasn't any kids.*

Why is a single person like borrowed money?   *ANS: Because he is alone.*

What is the end of celibacy?   *ANS: A cy (a sigh).*

Why is a grasshopper like a grass widow?   *ANS: Because he will jump at the first chance.*

Why should a timid bachelor marry a widow?   *ANS: Because then he can't marry amiss.*

What is the most suitable dower for a widow?   *ANS: Wi-dower.*

Why doesn't a bachelor take a partner with him on the ocean of life?   *ANS: Because he is afraid it might not be pacific.*

Why ought spinsters to stay at home in fine weather? *ANS: Because society does not approve of their having a little son and heir until they are married.*

Why does a bachelor who has a counterfeit half dollar passed to him want to get married?   *ANS: Because he wants to get a better half.*

11

Music and Art;
Entertainment and Amusement

MUSIC

Musical Instruments

Why are pianos so noble?   *ANS: Because they are upright, grand, and square.*

A man was locked in a room which had nothing in it except a piano. How did he get out?   *ANS: He played the piano until he found the right key.*

When you listen to your little brother's drum, why are you like a just judge?   *ANS: Because you hear both sides.*

How do we know that phonographs have been to jail? *ANS: They all have records.*

Why is the music of a grind organ considered classical? *ANS: Because it is a production by handle.*

Why is a disreputable alehouse like two of the chief instruments in an orchestra?   *ANS: Because it is a base and vile inn.*

What musical instrument has had an honorary degree conferred upon it?   *ANS: Fiddle, D. D.*

What musical instrument is bound to make false notes? *ANS: Lyre.*

What musical instrument is a corn-cob?   *ANS: Corn-et.*

Musical Keys

What is the best musical motto?   *ANS: B-sharp and B-natural, but never B-flat.*

What musical key makes a good army officer?   *ANS: A-sharp major.*

What is the keynote of good manners?   *ANS: B-natural.*

What musical key cannot vote?   *ANS: A-minor.*

Why are sidewalks in winter like music?   *ANS: Because if you don't C-sharp, you will B-flat.*

Music: General and Miscellaneous

Why is music cheaper on Sunday than during the week? *ANS: Because during the week you get it by the piece, but on Sunday you get it by the choir.*

When can you be said literally to "drink in" music?   *ANS: When you have a pianoforte (piano-for-tea).*

What pets make the loudest music?   *ANS: Trum-pets.*

Why is it vulgar to play and sing by yourself?   *ANS: Because it is so-lo.*

Why is a list of celebrated musicians like a saucepan? *ANS: Because it is incomplete without a Handel.*

Why was Rossini a very unnatural son?   *ANS: Because he made a Stab-at Mater.*

Why does "the British Matron" prefer old songs?   *ANS: Because she greatly objects to nudities (new ditties).*

What sort of tunes do we all enjoy most?   *ANS: For-tunes, made up of bank notes.*

Why is a song by a very poor singer like an old man's head? *ANS: Because it is likely to be terribly bawled.*

What change of identity did the *Beggar's Opera* effect? *ANS: It made Gay rich and Rich gay.*

Why is the nurse of an insane ward like a popular opera star?   *ANS: Because everybody is crazy about her.*

A little girl had a teddy bear. The bear's glass eyes had fallen out and had been replaced in such a way as to be crooked. The girl began calling the bear "Gladly," and explained that she got the name from a Sunday-school song. What is the name of the song?   *ANS: "Gladly the Cross I'd Bear."*

FINE ART AND PHOTOGRAPHY

What does an artist best like to draw?   *ANS: His salary.*

What city of the world do artists make the most drawings of? *ANS: Cork.*

Why is a marine painter like a large ship?   *ANS: Because he draws so much water.*

Why do architects make good actors?   *ANS: Because they are good at drawing houses.*

Why is a bad picture like weak tea?   *ANS: Because it is not well drawn.*

Why, when you paint a man's portrait, may you be described as stepping into his shoes?   *ANS: Because you make his features (feet yours).*

Why, if a man has a gallery of paintings, may you properly pick his pockets?   *ANS: Because he has pict-ures.*

Why is a portrait of Queen Elizabeth like a wager that is neither won nor lost?   *ANS: Because it is a drawn Bet.*

Why was Hiram Powers, the sculptor, one of the cheekiest men that ever lived?   *ANS: Because he unblushingly sent to be exhibited a poor "Greek Slave," whom he had chiselled out of all her clothes.*

Why are photographers the most uncivil of people?   *ANS: Because when we make application for a copy of our portrait, they always reply with a negative.*

Is there anything a man with a camera cannot take?   *ANS: Yes, a hint.*

Why is photography antagonistic to portrait painting? *ANS: Because it is a pho-to-graphic art.*

THEATER AND PUBLIC ENTERTAINMENT

Why is a theater such a sad place?   *ANS: Because all the seats are in tiers.*

What is the coldest place in a theater?   *ANS: Z-row.*

What are the best seats in a theater?   *ANS: Re-ceipts.*

What are stage buildings made of?   *ANS: Sham-rocks.*

Why is an actor better dead than living?
ANS: When alive he scarce a living can get,
When he's dead he fills both box and pit.

Why is a race at a circus like a big conflagration?   *ANS: Because the heat is in tents.*

SPORTS, GAMES, AND RECREATION

What is a great game on a small scale?   *ANS: Cricket on the hearth.*

What well-known game is an invisible color?   *ANS: Blind-man's buff.*

What is the best game for a Christmas party?   *ANS: A haunch of venison.*

What plays when it works, and works when it plays? *ANS: A fountain.*

Why is a defeated team like wool?   *ANS: Because it is worsted.*

Why are athletic records such brittle things?   *ANS: Because they cannot be lowered without breaking.*

When is a prize cup most likely to run?   *ANS: When it is chased.*

Why is it hard to get a baseball game started in the afternoon?   *ANS: Because the bats like to sleep in the daytime.*

Why is a baseball game like a cake?   *ANS: Because its success depends on the batter.*

Why is a baseball game like yesterday?   *ANS: Because it is a pastime.*

How can a baseball game end in a score of four to two without a man reaching first base?   *ANS: The players are all women.*

Why did Babe Ruth and Lou Gehrig make so much money? *ANS: Because a good batter makes good dough.*

Why is tennis such a noisy game?   *ANS: Because every player raises a racket.*

Why is a young lady like a very bad batsman in a game of cricket?   *ANS: Because she comes out at her very first ball.*

What animal do you look like when you go in swimming? *ANS: A little bare.*

Why is an ex-pugilist like a beehive?   *ANS: An ex-pugilist is an ex-pounder; an expounder is a commentator; a common 'tater is an Irish 'tater; an Irish 'tater is a specked 'tater; a spectator is a beholder; and a bee-holder is a beehive.*

Why is a boy turning a somersault no longer a boy?   *ANS: Because he is turning turtle.*

Why is a very amusing man like a very bad shot?   *ANS: Because he keeps the game alive.*

What paper should make the best kites?   *ANS: Flypaper.*

What did the big firecracker say to the little firecracker? *ANS: "My pop's bigger than your pop."*

Why is dancing like new milk?   *ANS: Because it strengthens the calves.*

What is the most suitable dance to wind up a frolic? *ANS: A reel.*

What dance do bakers prefer?   *ANS: A-bun-dance.*

Why is the game of blindman's buff like sympathy?   *ANS: Because it is a fellow feeling for another.*

Why are playing cards like wolves?   *ANS: Because they come in packs.*

Why is a group of convicts like a deck of cards?   *ANS: Because there is a knave in every suit.*

Why is a pack of only fifty-one cards, sent home, like one of fifty-two cards?   *ANS: Because it is sent incomplete.*

In what respect is matrimony a game of cards?   *ANS: A woman has a heart, a man takes it with a diamond, and after that her hand is his.*

Why is playing chess better than playing cards?   *ANS: Because you play chess with two bishops, but cards with four knaves.*

STORIES, HUMOR, AND PUZZLES

Why is a joke less durable than a church bell?   *ANS: Because after it has been told a few times it is worn out.*

Why is a poor joke like a broken pencil?   *ANS: Because it has no point.*

Why is a joke like a coconut?   *ANS: Because it's no good until it is cracked.*

Why is it best to tell a story with a hammer?   *ANS: To make it more striking.*

What should one do if he splits his sides laughing?   *ANS: Run until he gets a stitch in them.*

Why do people laugh up their sleeves?   *ANS: Because that is where their funnybones are.*

I know something that will tickle you. What?   *ANS: A feather.*

Why is a crossword puzzle like a quarrel?   *ANS: Because one word leads to another.*

Why is a person reading these conundrums like a man condemned to undergo a military execution?   *ANS: Because he is pretty sure to be riddled to death.*

Why are riddles that cannot be answered like a man disappointed by his visitors?   *ANS: Because there is a host put out and not one guessed.*

Did you ever hear the story of the red-hot poker?   *ANS: You couldn't grasp it.*

Did you ever hear the story about the two holes in the ground?   *ANS: Well, well.*

Did you ever hear the story of the new roof?   *ANS: It's over your head.*

Did you ever hear the story of the dirty window?   *ANS: You couldn't see through it.*

12

Money, Finance, and Business

COINS AND BILLS

Which is more valuable, a paper dollar or a silver dollar? *ANS: The paper dollar, because when you put it into your pocket you double it, and when you take it out you find it in creases.*

Which is better, an old five-dollar bill or a new one? *ANS: Any five-dollar bill is better than a one-dollar bill.*

Why is gooseberry jam like counterfeit money? *ANS: Because it is not currant.*

If you see a counterfeit coin on the street, why should you pick it up? *ANS: Because you might be arrested for passing it.*

Why is a penny like a rooster on a fence? *ANS: Because its head is on one side and its tail on the other.*

A nickel and a dime were crossing a bridge and the nickel fell off. Why didn't the dime fall too? *ANS: Because it had more cents than the nickel.*

Why is an empty purse always the same? *ANS: Because there is never any change in it.*

Why does everybody else have more money in his pocket than you have? *ANS: Because you never have any money in his pocket.*

What should you do if you had a dime and a buggy top? *ANS: Spend the dime for a fine-toothed comb and comb the bugs out.*

What coin doubles in value when half is deducted?   *ANS: A half dollar.*

What is the difference between a new five-cent piece and an old-fashioned quarter?   *ANS: Twenty cents.*

DEBT AND CREDIT

Why should buying trousers on credit be considered dishonorable?   *ANS: Because they are breeches of trust.*

What is the debtor's favorite tree?   *ANS: The will-owe.*

When may a man be said to be over head and ears in debt?   *ANS: When he hasn't paid for his wig.*

Why are pawnbrokers like the Salvation Army?   *ANS: Because they take great interest in serving the poor.*

Why is a pawnbroker like a drunkard?   *ANS: Because he takes the pledge but cannot always keep it.*

PROFIT AND LOSS; GAMBLING

What is the surest way to double your dollar?   *ANS: Fold it.*

What money brings the most substantial interest?   *ANS: Matri-mony.*

Who is it that always has a number of movements on foot for making money?   *ANS: A dancing master.*

Why is a sovereign gained like a guinea?   *ANS: Because it is one pound won.*

When does an Englishman double his money?   *ANS: When he makes one pound two every day.*

Why is a lucky gambler an agreeable fellow?   *ANS: Because he has such winning ways.*

What is the best bet ever made?   *ANS: Alphabet.*

Why is the condition of a sick man improved by wagering only a nickel?   *ANS: Because it makes him a little bettor.*

Why is a man who does not go to the races and bet just as bad as one who does?   *ANS: Because he is no bettor.*

O and P run a race; we bet on O, but P wins; why are we then like the Latakia tobacco which is given to us when we ask for burley?   *ANS: Because it is wrong to back O.*

WEALTH, POVERTY, AND CHARITY

Although great wealth is said to harden the heart, what is every millionaire sure to be?   *ANS: A capital fellow.*

Why should you ride a mule if you want to get rich?   *ANS: Because you are no sooner on than you are better off.*

Why is a vagrant like a balloon?   *ANS: Because he has no visible means of support.*

Where should you feel for the poor?   *ANS: In your pocket.*

Why is giving coal the best form of charity?   *ANS: Because it makes the receivers' grate full.*

When is charity like a top?   *ANS: When it begins to hum.*

BANKING, FINANCE, AND BUSINESS

Why do bankers always hear the latest financial news? *ANS: Because they have cash-iers.*

What are stocks?   *ANS: What a great many of the rogues who deal in them ought to be put into.*

What is the best system of bookkeeping?   *ANS: Never lend them.*

What kind of face does an auctioneer like best?   *ANS: One that is for bidding.*

If I buy four pieces of candy for a British penny and give one of them away, why am I like a telescope?   *ANS: Because I make a far-thing present.*

Why is coal the most contradictory substance known to commerce?   *ANS: Because when purchased it goes to the cellar.*

Why was the moron able to buy ice at half price?   *ANS: Because it was melted.*

If a ton of coal costs $6.50, what will a cord of firewood come to?   *ANS: Ashes.*

Smith gave Forty eight dollars for a horse, and then sold it for sixty dollars. What was his profit?   *ANS: Fifty-two dollars. The first seller's name was Forty.*

If you can buy eight eggs for twenty-six cents, how many can you buy for a cent and a quarter?   *ANS: Eight.*

If butter is fifty cents a pound in Chicago, what are window-panes in Detroit?   *ANS: Glass.*

MISCELLANEOUS

Why is a spendthrift's purse like a thundercloud?   *ANS: Because it is continually lightening.*

What is the easiest thing for a stingy man to part with? *ANS: A comb.*

Why is an avaricious man like one with a short memory? *ANS: Because he is always for getting.*

Why does a young woman prefer her mother's fortune to her father's? *ANS: Because, while she likes patrimony, she likes matrimony better.*

How can a man make his money go a long way? *ANS: By contributing to foreign missions.*

What do you call a man who is always wiring for money? *ANS: An electrician.*

13

Plants and Their Fruits

FLOWERS, SHRUBS, AND VINES

What flower is what the man out in the cold did to his nose?
ANS: Bluet.

What flower is what the Scotch girl said when she was asked
to walk the tightrope?   *ANS: Canna.*

What flower is what the landlord does when he turns off the
heat?   *ANS: Freesia.*

What flower is Hero's exclamation?   *ANS: O-Leander.*

What flower is what the woman said to the tramp?   *ANS:
Begonia.*

What rose is high in the public esteem?   *ANS: Heroes.*

What vine produces meat?   *ANS: Bovine.*

What did the big rose say to the little rose?   *ANS: "Hiya,
Bud."*

What did the rose say to the sun?   *ANS: "Blow me."*

What did Jack Frost say when he kissed the violet?   *ANS:
"Wilt thou?" and it wilted.*

TREES

When the poet asked the woodman to "spare that tree,"
why did he expect his request to be granted?   *ANS: Because he knew the woodman was a good feller.*

What ailment is the oak tree most subject to?   *ANS: A corn.*

What tree bears the most toothsome fruit?   *ANS: Dentistry.*

Sam Patch would go to the tallest trees, take off his boots, and jump over them. How was that?   *ANS: He would jump over his boots.*

Why may the proprietor of a forest not fell his own timber? *ANS: Because no one is permitted to cut when it is his own deal.*

If you should plant a puppy, what kind of tree would come up?   *ANS: A dogwood.*

What tree is most suggestive of kissing?   *ANS: Yew (you).*

GRASS AND GRAIN

Why is hay like spectacles?   *ANS: Because it is for-age.*

Why is a field of grass like a person older than you?   *ANS: Because it is past-ur-age.*

What kind of grain is usually sown at night?   *ANS: Wild oats.*

How can you make fifteen bushels of corn from one bushel of corn?   *ANS: Pop it.*

If a farmer can raise fifty bushels of corn in dry weather, what can he raise in wet weather?   *ANS: An umbrella.*

What is the color of a grass plot covered with snow?   *ANS: Invisible green. ("Invisible green": A certain color, bluish-green or yellowish-green in hue.)*

In one corner of a field there are 7 3/4 haystacks; in the second corner there are 3 4/7 haystacks; in the third corner

2 1/7 haystacks; in the fourth corner 1 2/7 haystacks. When the farmer puts all these haystacks together, how many haystacks will he have?   *ANS: One.*

PLANTS IN GENERAL

Why are seeds when sown like gateposts?   *ANS: Because they propagate.*

How far can you go into the woods?   *ANS: As far as the middle; after that you will be going out.*

Why is it easy to practice rotation of crops on the prairies? *ANS: Because of the frequency of the whirlwinds there.*

How did the garden laugh at the gardener?   *ANS: It said, "Hoe, hoe."*

Why is a gardener the most extraordinary man in the world? *ANS: Because he has more business on earth than any other man; he has good grounds for what he does; he is master of the mint; sets his own thyme; has more boughs than the President of the United States; and, better still, he can raise his own celery every year.*

Why is it more dangerous to go to the woods in the spring than at any other time?   *ANS: Because in the spring the grass has blades, the flowers have pistils, the leaves shoot, the cowslips about, and the bulrush is out.*

FRUITS AND VEGETABLES

What fruit do we get from the electric light plant?   *ANS: Currents.*

What kind of fruit is like a statue?   *ANS: A fig, because it is F-I-G (effigy).*

If I were to see you riding on a donkey, what fruit should I be reminded of? *ANS: A pair.*

When are apples like printer's type? *ANS: When they are in pie.*

If Bob had a whole apple and Tom had only a bite, what should Tom do? *ANS: Scratch it.*

What is the reddest side of an apple? *ANS: The outside.*

How can you divide nineteen apples absolutely equally among seven small boys? *ANS: Make them into apple-sauce, and measure it out very carefully.*

What did the apple say to the apple pie? *ANS: "You've got a crust."*

When are two apples alike? *ANS: When they are pared.*

When an apple wanted to fight a banana, why did the banana run away? *ANS: Because it was yellow.*

What did the mother strawberry say to the baby strawberry? *ANS: "Junior, don't get into a jam."*

Why are strawberries in winter like a pair of antlered bucks? *ANS: Because they are too dear.*

What did one peach say to another? *ANS: "How did we ever get out on such a limb?"*

Why does a watermelon have so much water in it? *ANS: Because it is planted in the spring.*

When is a man like a green gooseberry? *ANS: When a woman makes a fool of him. ("Gooseberry fool": A dessert made of stewed gooseberries, sugar, and whipped cream.)*

Why do people preserve vegetables more than they used to? *ANS: Because they can.*

What vegetable makes up the alphabet? *ANS: Lettuce (letters).*

What is the largest vegetable?   *ANS: A policeman's beat.*

What vegetable needs a plumber?   *ANS: Leek.*

What vegetable should every poultryman own?   *ANS: Eggplant.*

What herb cures all diseases?   *ANS: Thyme.*

Why is an onion like a ringing bell?   *ANS: Because peel follows peel.*

Why is a man who has nothing to boast about but his ancestors like a potato plant?   *ANS: Because the best things that belong to him are under ground.*

Why are potato plants like mended trousers?   *ANS: Because you see them in patches.*

What fruit is what happens when a girl's plans for a runaway match are frustrated?   *ANS: Cantaloupe.*

How many peas in a pint?   *ANS: One P.*

14
Time

Timepieces

What part of a clock has been used before?   *ANS: Second hand.*

What part of a clock is something you should not take in vain?   *ANS: Maker's name.*

How long will an eight-day clock run without winding? *ANS: It won't run at all without winding.*

When do clocks talk the most?   *ANS: When they are well wound up.*

Why does a clock never strike thirteen?   *ANS: It hasn't the face to do so.*

If a man should smash a clock, would he be accused of killing time?   *ANS: Not if the clock struck first.*

Why is a clock unlike a corporation?   *ANS: Because it goes on with its business after it is completely wound up.*

Why should a clock never be placed at the head of the stairs?   *ANS: Because it might run down and strike one.*

A little wooden man stands on top of a clock. Every time he hears the clock strike once he jumps twice. The clock strikes every hour. How many times does the man jump in twenty-four hours?   *ANS: None, for a wooden man cannot hear the clock.*

When is a very angry man like a clock showing fifty-nine minutes past twelve?   *ANS: When he is just about to strike one.*

Why did the moron throw his clock out the window? *ANS: He liked to see time fly.*

Why can you never buy a new chronometer?   *ANS: Because it must always be a second-hand one.*

Why is a watch like a thing-um-a-bob?   *ANS: Because it is a watch-you-may-call-it.*

Why should you always carry a watch when crossing a desert? *ANS: Because it has a spring in it.*

When is it difficult to get one's watch out of one's pocket? *ANS: When it's ticking there.*

When should a man wear a large watch?   *ANS: When he wants to have a big time.*

When may a man be said to possess a vegetable timepiece? *ANS: When he gets up at eight o'clock (a potato clock).*

Time of Day

What time is it when the clock strikes thirteen?   *ANS: Time to have the clock repaired.*

If a man should give one son fifteen cents and another ten cents, what time would it be?   *ANS: A quarter to two.*

What time is it when you see a monkey scratching with his left hand?   *ANS: Five after one.*

What time is it when a pie is equally divided among four hungry boys?   *ANS: A quarter to one.*

If the postmaster went to the circus and a lion ate him, what time would it be?   *ANS: Ate P.M. (eight P.M.).*

At what time by the clock is a pun most effective?   *ANS: When it strikes one.*

What is a good way to kill time in the winter?   *ANS: Sleigh it.*

Why is it that there is not a moment that we can call our own?   *ANS: Because the minutes are not hours.*

What is the best way to make the hours go fast?   *ANS: Use the spur of the moment.*

What animal keeps the best time?   *ANS: A watchdog.*

Why is it no offense to conspire in the evening?   *ANS: What is treasonable is reasonable after T (tea).*

How do you know when night is nigh?   *ANS: When the T (tea) is taken away.*

DAYS, WEEKS, MONTHS, AND SEASONS

What is so rare as a day in June?   *ANS: Some days in March are pretty raw.*

Which is the strongest day of the week?   *ANS: Sunday, because all the rest are week-days.*

Where does Friday come before Thursday?   *ANS: In the dictionary.*

What is the best day for making pancakes?   *ANS: Fri-day.*

Why are the days long in summer and short in winter?   *ANS: Because heat expands things, and cold contracts them.*

When day breaks, what becomes of the pieces?   *ANS: They go into morning.*

Why is there no such thing as a whole day?   *ANS: Because every day begins by breaking.*

What day of the year is a command to go forward?   *ANS: March fourth.*

Why should soldiers be especially tired on the first of April? *ANS: Because they have just finished a March of thirty-one days.*

How many weeks belong to the year?   *ANS: Forty-six; the other six are only Lent.*

Where was time raised?   *ANS: In the laps of ages.*

What are the embers of the expiring year?   *ANS: Nov-ember and Dec-ember.*

In what month do women talk the least?   *ANS: In the shortest month, February.*

Why does summer go so quickly?   *ANS: Because there is often an evening mist.*

15

Transportation and Communication

RAILWAYS

What happens to a man who starts home to dinner and misses his train?   *ANS: He catches it when he gets home.*

Why does a freight car need no locomotive?   *ANS: Because the freight makes the cargo.*

Why should one never complain about the price of a railroad ticket?   *ANS: Because it is a fare thing.*

Why is a railroad section hand like a hunted bear in the mountains?   *ANS: Because he makes tracks for his life.*

Why can a railroad locomotive not sit down?   *ANS: Because it has a tender behind.*

When is it hard to catch a train?   *ANS: When the train has a head start.*

What motive did the inventor of railways have in view? *ANS: Locomotive.*

Why is a railroad exceedingly patriotic?   *ANS: Because it is bound to the country with the strongest ties.*

SHIPS

Sailors

When is a sailor like a beach?   *ANS: When he's ashore.*

When is a sailor not a sailor?   *ANS: When he's aloft.*

When else is a sailor not a sailor?   *ANS: When he's aboard.*

When is a sailor like a corpse?   *ANS: When he's in the shrouds.*

Why is a love of the ocean like curiosity?   *ANS: Because it has sent many a boy to sea.*

Why do sailors working in brigs make bad servants?   *ANS: Because it is impossible for a man to serve two masters well.*

Why are sailors bad horsemen?   *ANS: Because they ride on the main.*

If a disabled sailor goes into business, why must it be retail business?   *ANS: Because he cannot be a whole sailor.*

When I looked through the window I saw a ship sailing.
    Now w'at is the captain's name?
Though I've told you before I ask you once more,
    W'at is the captain's name?
ANS: Watt.

Why should a sailor be the best authority as to what is going on in the moon?   *ANS: Because he has been to sea.*

What Ship?

What ship has two mates but no captain?   *ANS: Court-ship.*

What ship held only twelve persons?   *ANS: Apostleship.*

What ship has no soft berths?   *ANS: Hardship.*

What ship carries more passengers than the *Queen Mary?*
ANS: Courtship.

What ship is always fastened to a peer?   *ANS: Lordship.*

What ship is always managed by more than one person?
ANS: Partnership.

What ship is never overloaded?   *ANS: Statesmanship.*

What ship is one on which no woman objects to embark? *ANS: Courtship.*

Ships: Miscellaneous

Why is the rudder of a steamship like a hangman?   *ANS: Because it has a stern duty to perform.*

Why is a ship like a woman?   *ANS: Because she is often tender to a man-of-war; often running after a smack; often attached to a buoy; and frequently making up to a pier.*

Why is the mainmast of a ship like the first chicken of a brood?   *ANS: Because it is a little ahead of the main hatch.*

Why is a ferryboat like a good rule?   *ANS: Because it works both ways.*

Why can a New York tugboat not go straight?   *ANS: Because sometimes it tows in and sometimes tows out.*

When is a boat like a heap of snow?   *ANS: When it's adrift.*

What does the steamer *Queen Mary* weigh just before leaving New York harbor?   *ANS: She weighs anchor.*

If you were fishing in Boston harbor and a hostile gunboat should appear, what would be the best thing to do?   *ANS: Pull up your line and sinker.*

Why is the director of a children's playground like a stranded vessel?   *ANS: Because he runs a ground.*

When is a ship's anchor like a chicken? *ANS: When it's afoul.*

Where does the captain of a ship keep his poultry?   *ANS: In the hatchway.*

When has a woman going to Europe by ship most reason to feel flat?   *ANS: When she's aboard.*

What was the captain's order when all the passengers were heaving?   *ANS: For the ship to heave to.*

When does a boat show affection?   *ANS: When it hugs the shore.*

When may a ship be said to be absurdly in love?   *ANS: When she is h'anchoring after a heavy swell.*

When is she actively in love?   *ANS: When she seeks a mate.*

When is she weakly in love?   *ANS: When she rests on the bosom of a little cove.*

TRANSPORTATION: GENERAL AND MISCELLANEOUS

When does a girl become a two-wheeled vehicle?   *ANS: When she is a little sulky.*

What is better than presence of mind in an automobile accident?   *ANS: Absence of body.*

What make of automobile is what the woman asked when she bought a hen?   *ANS: Chevrolet.*

What comes with an auto, is of no use to an auto, and yet the auto cannot run without it?   *ANS: Noise.*

Why is a man who has fallen off a tree, and is determined to go up again, like a man emigrating?   *ANS: He is going to try another climb (clime).*

What is the hardest thing about learning to ride a bicycle?   *ANS: The pavement.*

Why do some persons press the elevator button with the thumb, and others with the forefinger?   *ANS: To signal the elevator.*

Why is a city bus like the heart of a coquette?   *ANS: Because there is always room for one more to be taken in.*

Why is a girl named Ann, when she travels from London to Kew by a public conveyance, likely to prove a burden to her friends?   *ANS: Because she is Ann in Kew Bus (an incubus).*

Why do taxi drivers prefer tall women passengers to short ones?   *ANS: Because the higher the fare, the better they like it.*

Why should a taxi driver be brave?   *ANS: Because none but the brave deserve the fair.*

When is a cabman like a carpenter's implement?   *ANS: When he's a screw driver. ("Screw": A worn-out or broken-down horse.)*

Why are coachmen like clouds?   *ANS: Because they hold the reins.*

What bridge creates the most anxiety?   *ANS: A suspension bridge.*

If the Forth Bridge were to collapse, what would they do?   *ANS: Construct a fifth.*

Why is Brooklyn Bridge like merit?   *ANS: Because it is often passed over.*

Why is Brooklyn Bridge like a firm in trouble?   *ANS: Because it is suspended.*

What do you always notice running along the streets in a town?   *ANS: The curb.*

When are roads like corpses?   *ANS: When they are mended.*

What makes a road broad?   *ANS: The letter B.*

COMMUNICATION

What are the quickest ways of spreading news? *ANS: Telephone, telegraph, and tell-a-woman.*

Why can we send no more dispatches to Washington? *ANS: Because he is dead.*

Why is opening a letter like taking a very queer method of getting into a room? *ANS: Because it is breaking through the sealing.*

If a telephone and a piece of paper should run a race, which would win? *ANS: The telephone, because the paper would always remain stationery.*

Why is a sheet of postage stamps like distant relatives? *ANS: Because they are but slightly connected.*

Why do women make good post-office clerks? *ANS: Because they know how to manage the males.*

Why is a news broadcaster like an Irish vegetable? *ANS: Because he is a commentator.*

What did one little ink drop ask another little ink drop? *ANS: Are all your relatives in the pen too?*

16

Certain Classes of People

CHILDREN AND YOUTH

Why is a newborn babe like a little dog's tail?   *ANS: Because it was never seen before.*

Why is an infant like a diamond?   *ANS: Because it's a dear little thing.*

When is a baby not a baby?   *ANS: When it's a little cross.*

Why is a newborn baby like a storm?   *ANS: Because it begins with a squall.*

Why is a baby like wheat?   *ANS: Because it is first cradled, then thrashed, and finally becomes the flower of the family.*

Why is a baby boy always welcome?   *ANS: Because he never comes a miss.*

When is a baby like a breakfast cup?   *ANS: When it's a tee-thing.*

Why are babies like troubles?   *ANS: Because they grow bigger by nursing.*

Have you ever heard of a baby raised on elephant's milk? *ANS: Yes, a baby elephant.*

Who is bigger, Mrs. Bigger or her baby?   *ANS: The baby is a little Bigger.*

Why is a woman with baby twins like a sentinel on duty? *ANS: Because she goes with loaded arms.*

Prove that a baby is not worth two cents.   *ANS: A baby is a crier. A crier is a messenger. A messenger is one sent. One cent is not worth two cents. Therefore a baby is not worth two cents.*

Why is a dirty child like flannel?   *ANS: Because it shrinks from washing.*

A woman had five children and half of them were boys. How could that be?   *ANS: The other half were boys, too.*

Do you believe in clubs for young people?   *ANS: Only when kindness fails.*

Whom do children dislike the most?   *ANS: The women who bore them.*

When is a boy not a boy?   *ANS: When he's a regular brick.*

When is a boy not a boy?   *ANS: When he's abed.*

When is a boy in a pantry like a poacher?   *ANS: When he walks into the preserves. ("Walk into": To eat greedily.)*

CERTAIN RACES OR NATIONALITIES

Why is a Zulu belle like a prophet?   *ANS: Because she has very little on her in her own country.*

Why is a colored woman like a doorway?   *ANS: Because she's a Negress.*

Why is a colored man necessarily a conjurer?   *ANS: Because he's a Negro man, sir.*

Why are quinine and gentian like the Germans?   *ANS: Because they are two tonics.*

Why is a barefooted boy like an Eskimo?   *ANS: Because he wears no shoes.*

Why do Irish peasants wear capes?   *ANS: To "cape" them warm.*

Why are the Irish poor like a carpet?   *ANS: Because they are kept down by tax.*

What is an Irishman's definition of a lake?   *ANS: A hole in the tay-kettle.*

When is a Scotchman like a donkey?   *ANS: When he strolls along his banks and braes.*

CERTAIN TRADES AND VOCATIONS

What Trade or Vocation?

What trade is one in which a man will never make a cent except by sticking to it?   *ANS: Bill-posting.*

What trade does a little tin dog follow?   *ANS: Tin-cur.*

What kind of business never makes progress?   *ANS: The stationery business.*

When may a man properly be said to be immersed in his business?   *ANS: When he gives a swimming lesson.*

Who earns his living without doing a day's work?   *ANS: A night watchman.*

What tradesman should always be prosperous?   *ANS: The sausage maker, for he always makes both ends meat.*

What should be the best profession for a student who is always at the foot of his class?   *ANS: Chiropodist.*

What man's business is best when things are dullest?   *ANS: A knife sharpener.*

What professional man generally works with a will?   *ANS: A lawyer.*

What man makes his living only at put-up jobs? *ANS: A paper hanger.*

What vocation should one follow who wants to cut a figure in the world? *ANS: Sculptor.*

A Few Specified Trades

Why are blacksmiths undesirable citizens? *ANS: Because they forge and steel daily.*

Why is a chandler like an exposed villain? *ANS: Because all his wicked works are brought to light.*

Why may carpenters reasonably believe there is no such thing as stone? *ANS: Because they never saw it.*

Why is a retired carpenter like a lecturer? *ANS: Because he is an ex-planer.*

When are electricians most successful? *ANS: When they make good connections.*

What is necessary to a farmer to assist him? *ANS: A system.*

How could a good fireman lose his job? *ANS: He might go to blazes too fast.*

When does the hotel boy become a porter? *ANS: When he reaches the lug-age.*

When should a publican go to an iron foundry? *ANS: When he wants a barmaid.*

Why is a real-estate man not a man of words? *ANS: Because he's a man of deeds.*

What kind of servants are best for hotels? *ANS: The inn-experienced.*

Why are soldiers in the U.S. Army not going to have bayonets any longer? *ANS: Because they are long enough.*

Why do pioneers go ahead of the army?   *ANS: To axe the way.*

When is a soldier not a whole soldier?   *ANS: When he is in quarters.*

Why is a woodman very inconsistent?   *ANS: Because he cuts a tree down, and then cuts it up.*

CERTAIN TRAITS OR HABITS

Why must a dishonest man stay indoors?   *ANS: So no one will ever find him out.*

Why is an honest friend like orange chips?   *ANS: Because he's candid.*

What men are most aboveboard in their movements? *ANS: Chessmen.*

Why is a false friend like your shadow?   *ANS: Because he follows you only in sunshine.*

Why is troy weight like an unconscientious person?   *ANS: Because it has no scruples.*

Why are smoking pipes all humbugs?   *ANS: Because the best of them are meer-schaums.*

Can you tell me why
A hypocrite's eye
Can better descry
Than you or I
On how many toes
A pussycat goes?

ANS: *The eye of deceit*
Can best counterfeit
And so, I suppose,
Can best count 'er toes.

What kind of vice is it that people dislike if they are ever so bad?   *ANS: Ad-vice.*

Who is the oldest lunatic on record?   *ANS: Time out of mind.*

Why did the moron throw all his nails away?   *ANS: Because the heads were on the wrong end.*

What is the height of folly?   *ANS: Spending one's last dollar on a purse.*

Why is a blockhead deserving of promotion?   *ANS: Because he is equal to any post.*

Why is a prudent man like a pin?   *ANS: Because his head prevents his going too far.*

What are the most unsociable things in the world?   *ANS: Milestones, for you never see two of them together.*

What should we give people who are too breezy?   *ANS: The air.*

What is more to be admired than a promising young man? *ANS: A paying one.*

Why is a man who is always complaining really the easiest man to satisfy?   *ANS: Because nothing satisfies him.*

When is it a good thing to lose your temper?   *ANS: When it is a bad one.*

Why are dudes no longer imported into this country from England?   *ANS: Because a Yankee-doodle-doo.*

Why are the Royal Academicians the greatest swells ever known?   *ANS: Because Solomon, even in all his glory, was not R.A.'d (arrayed) like one of these.*

Three copycats were sitting on a cliff and one jumped off. How many were left?   *ANS: None, because they were all copycats.*

What chasm often separates friends?   *ANS: Sarcasm.*

Where lies the path of duty?   *ANS: Through the custom-house.*

If you woke up in the night feeling sad, what would you do?
ANS: Look on the bed for a comforter.

What is the best way to keep loafers from standing on street
corners?   *ANS: Give them chairs and let them sit down.*

When does a timid girl turn to stone?   *ANS: When she
becomes a little bolder.*

Why should you always remain calm when you encounter
cannibals?   *ANS: It is better not to get into a stew.*

Where can you always find sympathy?   *ANS: In the dictionary.*

Where does charity begin?   *ANS: At C (sea).*

When does a man feel girlish?   *ANS: When he makes his
maiden speech.*

RELATIVES

If a girl falls into a well, why can her brother not help her
out?   *ANS: Because he cannot be a brother and assist her
too.*

If a boy ate his father and mother, what would that make
him?   *ANS: An orphan.*

Why did the moron lock his father in the refrigerator?
ANS: Because he likes cold pop.

If you add a father, a mother, and a baby, what do you get?
ANS: Two, and one to carry.

A beggar's brother died, but the man who died had no brother. How could that be?   *ANS: The beggar was a woman.*

Two Indians are standing on a hill, and one is the father of the other's son. What relation are the two Indians to each other?   *ANS: Husband and wife.*

Man, looking at a portrait: "Brothers and sisters have I none, but that man's father is my father's son." Who is the subject of the portrait?   *ANS: The son of the speaker.*

If Dick's father is John's son, what relation is Dick to John? *ANS: Dick is John's grandson.*

If your uncle's sister is not your aunt, what relation is she to you?   *ANS: Your mother.*

A big Indian and a little Indian were walking down the road. The little Indian was the son of the big Indian, yet the big Indian was not the father of the little Indian. Why? *ANS: The big Indian was the mother of the little Indian.*

It wasn't my sister, nor my brother, but still was the child of my father and mother. Who was it?   *ANS: Myself.*

What relation is a child to its own father when it is not its own father's son?   *ANS: Daughter.*

Which of your relatives are dependent upon you for a living? *ANS: Your uncles, aunts, and cousins, for without U they could not exist.*

ANY MAN; LIFE AND DEATH

Any Man

What is everyone in the world doing at the same time? *ANS: Growing older.*

At what time of life may a man be said to belong to the vegetable kingdom?   *ANS: When long experience has made him sage.*

When is it easiest to see through a man?   *ANS: When he has a pain in his stomach.*

What is the best way to turn people's heads?   *ANS: Go to church late.*

What kind of paper tells you who you are?   *ANS: Tissue.*

What is a man like who is in the middle of the Hudson River and can't swim?   *ANS: Like to be drowned.*

When is a subject beneath one's notice?   *ANS: When it is under consideration.*

When does a man stand a good chance of being completely sewn up?   *ANS: When he has a stitch in his side.*

What is better than to give credit where credit is due? *ANS: Give cash.*

> There was a man who was not born,
>   His father was not before him.
> He did not live, he did not die.
>   His epitaph is not o'er him.

ANS: A man by the name of Nott.

> As I was going down the lane,
> I met a man who was doing the same;
> He tipped his hat an' drew his cane,
> And in this riddle I've told you his name.

ANS: Andrew.

Life and Death

Is life worth living?   *ANS: It depends on the liver.*

What requires more philosophy than taking things as they come?   *ANS: Parting with things as they go.*

Why is life like a harness?   *ANS: Because there are traces of care, lines of trouble, bits of good fortune, breaches of good manners, bridled tongues, and everybody has a tug to get through.*

What is the end to which we all like to come?   *ANS: Dividend.*

Why is the soul like a thing of no consequence?   *ANS: Because it is immaterial.*

Why is death like a boy breaking your window?   *ANS: Because it puts an end to your pains.*

Why is a duel quickly managed?   *ANS: Because it takes only two seconds to arrange it.*

How can you get into a locked cemetery at night?   *ANS: Use a skeleton key.*

Why is a tin can tied to a dog's tail like death?   *ANS: Because it is bound to a cur.*

What did the moron do when he thought he was dying? *ANS: He moved to the living room.*

Why is a firecracker like death?   *ANS: Because it is a detonator (debt of nature).*

17

Various Paradoxes

SIZE, WEIGHT, AND MOTION

What grows bigger the more you contract it?   *ANS: Debt.*

What is lengthened by being cut at both ends?   *ANS: A ditch.*

What is big enough to hold a pig and small enough to hold in your hand?   *ANS: A pen.*

What is it that has neither length, breadth, nor thickness, yet can be felt?   *ANS: A kiss.*

What is bought by the yard, but worn out by the foot? *ANS: A carpet.*

What is it that increases the more it is shared with others? *ANS: Happiness.*

The more you take away from it the larger it becomes; the more you add to it the smaller it becomes. What is it? *ANS: A hole in the ground, or in a stocking.*

What is it from which you may take away the whole and still have some left, or take away some and have the whole left?   *ANS: The word WHOLESOME.*

What goes farther the slower it goes?   *ANS: Money.*

What goes from New York to Albany without moving? *ANS: The highway.*

What is always coming but never arrives?   *ANS: To-morrow.*

What always remains down even when it flies up in the air? *ANS: A feather.*

What is it that you cannot hold ten minutes, even though it is lighter than a feather?   *ANS: Your breath.*

What always weighs the same, whether larger or smaller? *ANS: A hole.*

With what would you fill a barrel to make it lighter than when it is empty?   *ANS: Holes.*

GIVE AND TAKE; LIKE AND DISLIKE

What is it that no one wishes to have, yet no one wishes to lose?   *ANS: A bald head.*

What is it that everyone wishes for, and yet wants to get rid of as soon as it is obtained?   *ANS: A good appetite.*

What is it that a woman looks for, but hopes not to find? *ANS: A hole in her stocking.*

> Formed long ago, yet made today,
>   I'm most employed while others sleep;
> What none would like to give away,
>   Yet no one likes to keep.

ANS: A bed.

What is it that everyone requires, that everyone gives, that everyone asks, and that very few take?   *ANS: Advice.*

What is it that is often given you, which you never have, yet which you often give up?   *ANS: A conundrum.*

Those who have me do not wish for me; those who have me do not wish to lose me; those who gain me have me no longer. What am I?   *ANS: A lawsuit.*

What is it that the man who makes does not need, the man who buys does not use for himself, and the person who uses does so without knowing it?   *ANS: A coffin.*

What is it that was given to you, belongs to you exclusively, and yet is used more by your friends than by yourself? *ANS: Your name.*

What is it that you must keep after giving it to someone else?   *ANS: Your word.*

What is it that someone else has to take before you can get it?   *ANS: Your photograph.*

What is it that we often return but never borrow?   *ANS: Thanks.*

OTHER PARADOXES

What is full of holes and yet holds water?   *ANS: A sponge.*

What can be right but never wrong?   *ANS: An angle.*

What has eyes and can't see and ears and can't hear, and can jump as high as Bunker Hill Monument?   *ANS: A dead cat.*

Why, a dead cat can't jump.   *ANS: What of it, neither can Bunker Hill Monument.*

What is always before you, yet you can never see it?   *ANS: Your future.*

How might you be completely sleepless for seven days and still not lack any rest?   *ANS: By sleeping at night.*

What are always drunk but never intoxicated?   *ANS: Toasts.*

What lives on its own substance and dies when it devours itself?   *ANS: A candle.*

As long as I eat, I live; but when I drink, I die.   *ANS: Fire.*

What is it that is put on the table, cut, and passed, but never eaten? *ANS: A deck of cards.*

What is black and white and red all over? *ANS: A newspaper.*

What else is black and white and red all over? *ANS: An embarrassed zebra.*

What grows less tired the more it works? *ANS: An automobile wheel.*

What gets wetter the more it dries? *ANS: A towel.*

What is that of which the common sort is best? *ANS: Sense.*

How can a man fall off a fifty-foot ladder and not be hurt? *ANS: By falling off the bottom rung.*

What is it that everyone, no matter how careful, overlooks? *ANS: His nose.*

Why is it that when you are looking for something you always find it in the last place in which you look? *ANS: Because you stop looking for it after you find it.*

What is it that God never saw, George Washington seldom saw, but you and I see every day? *ANS: An equal.*

What is the most paradoxical sign? *ANS: "To speak aloud is not allowed."*

What is it that occurs four times in every week, twice in every month, and only once in a year? *ANS: The letter E.*

When is a man not a man? *ANS: When he is a-shaving.*

When does a man cease to be a man? *ANS: When he turns into a lane.*

When is a man two men? *ANS: When he is beside himself.*

When is a woman not a woman?   *ANS: When she is a little pale.*

What is the best thing to make in a hurry?   *ANS: Haste.*

What is it that every child spends much time in making, yet no one can see when it is made?   *ANS: Noise.*

What is it that you break when you name it?   *ANS: Silence.*

What can be broken without being hit or dropped?   *ANS: A promise.*

I am the center of gravity, hold a capital situation in Vienna, and as I am foremost in every victory, am allowed by all to be in-valuable. Always out of tune, yet ever in voice; invisible, though clearly seen in the midst of a river. I have three associates in vice, and could name three who are in love with me. Still it is in vain you seek me, for I have long been in heaven, and even now lie embalmed in the grave. *ANS: The letter V. (VAR: What is the center of gravity?)*

What is it that stands aloft and regulates our daily movements, yet feels no interest in our concerns; directs us when to go, and when to come, yet cares not whether we attend or not; still, thus indifferent to our fate, often strikes a blow to urge us on, though we feel no resentment when the reproof is given?   *ANS: A clock.*

> Four jolly men sat down to play,
> And played all night till break of day;
> They played for cash and not for fun,
> With a separate score for every one;
> Yet when they came to square accounts,
> They all had made quite fair amounts!
> Can you this paradox explain?
> If no one lost, how could all gain?

ANS: They were musicians in a dance orchestra.

18

What Is It?

What does everyone have that he can always count on?
ANS: His fingers.

What is it that one needs most in the long run?   *ANS: His breath.*

What do we all put off till tomorrow?   *ANS: Our clothes when we go to bed.*

What are the most disagreeable articles for a man to have on hand?   *ANS: Handcuffs.*

What do you lose every time you stand up?   *ANS: Your lap.*

What is a country seat?   *ANS: A milking stool.*

What is hard to beat?   *ANS: A drum with a hole in it.*

What is a Western settler?   *ANS: A six-shooter.*

What is true to the last?   *ANS: A well-made shoe.*

What will stay hot longest in the refrigerator?   *ANS: Red pepper.*

What is it that a man can use for shaving, cleaning his clothes, and sleeping in?   *ANS: A razor, a brush, and a suit of pajamas.*

What are the most patient objects in the shape of humanity?
ANS: Statues.

What smells most in a drugstore?   *ANS: The nose.*

What sticketh closer than a brother?   *ANS: A postage stamp, by gum.*

If you tumbled downstairs, what would you fall against?
ANS: Against your will.

What was the greatest feat of strength ever performed?
ANS: Wheeling, West Virginia.

What are the two strangest modern happenings?   *ANS: A deaf-mute picked up a wheel and spoke, and a blind man picked up a hammer and saw.*

What is the best thing out?   *ANS: A conflagration.*

What always ends everything?   *ANS: The letter G.*

What is the hardest thing to deal with?   *ANS: An old deck of cards.*

What does a man think is more blessed to give than to receive?   *ANS: Advice, kicks, and pills.*

What will always bear looking into once more?   *ANS: A mirror.*

What is mind?   *ANS: No matter.*

What is matter?   *ANS: Never mind.*

What is the brightest idea of the day?   *ANS: Your eye, dear (idea).*

What is the greatest terrifier?   *ANS: Fire.*

What is better than an idea?   *ANS: You, dear.*

What occurs once in a minute, twice in a moment, and not once in a hundred years?   *ANS: The letter M.*

What is the most important thing in the world?   *ANS: The letter E, because it is first in everybody and everything.*

> Sometimes I am very sly;
> Other times a trade I ply;
> Over the billows swift I fly;
> Now pray tell me, what am I?

ANS: Craft.

I went to a field and couldn't get through it,
So I went to a school and learned how to do it.
ANS: Fence.

I am filled every morning and emptied every night, except once a year, when I am filled at night and emptied in the morning. What am I?   *ANS: A stocking.*

What is too much for one, enough for two, but nothing at all for three?   *ANS: A secret.*

Born at the same time as the world, destined to live as long as the world, and yet never five weeks old. What is it? *ANS: The moon.*

What runs around town all day and lies under the bed at night with its tongue hanging out?   *ANS: A shoe.*

Those who take me improve, be their task what it may,
Those who have me are sorrowful through the long day;
I am hated alike by the foolish and wise,
Yet without me none ever to eminence rise.
ANS: Pains.

What lives in winter, dies in summer, and grows with its root upward?   *ANS: An icicle.*

Though they catch me with a hook,
I'm more allied to bird than beast;
In form more like a snake I look,
Though having sixteen feet at least.
ANS: A perch.

If you pull it it's a cane, but if you push it it's a tent.
ANS: An umbrella.

On the hill sits a green house,
In the green house is a white house,
In the white house is a red house,
In the red house are a lot of little black and white men.
ANS: A watermelon.

What should you always keep because nobody else wants it?
ANS: Your temper.

Luke had it first, Paul had it last; boys never have it; girls have it but once; Miss Sullivan had it twice in the same place, but when she married Pat Murphy she never had it again.   *ANS: The letter L.*

> The beginning of eternity,
> The end of time and space,
> The beginning of every end,
> The end of every race.

ANS: The letter E.

> Little Nancy Etticoat
> Wears a white petticoat
> And a red nose;
> The longer she stands,
> The shorter she grows.

ANS: A candle.

What is that walks over the fields all day, and sits in the icebox at night?   *ANS: Milk.*

> Humpty Dumpty sat on a wall;
> Humpty Dumpty had a great fall.
> All the king's horses and all the king's men
> Couldn't put Humpty together again.

ANS: An egg.

What has two lookers, two hookers, four down-hangers, four upstanders, and a fly swatter?   *ANS: A cow.*

> Old Mother Twitchett, she had but one eye,
> And a great long tail that she let fly;
> And every time she went through a gap,
> She left a bit of her tail in the trap.

ANS: A needle and thread.

What has rods never used for fishing, poles on which you cannot hang flags, and perches upon which birds never rest?
ANS: An acre.

> We travel much, yet prisoners are,
>   And close confined to boot;
> We with the swiftest horse keep pace,
>   Yet always go on foot.

ANS: Spurs.

What we caught we threw away; what we could not catch, we kept.   *ANS: Fleas. (There is a legend that this riddle was given to the great Homer by a fisherman of Ios, and that Homer's death was a result of his chagrin over being unable to solve it. The story is sometimes attributed to Plutarch, but I have not found it in Plutarch's works.)*

> Twice ten are but six of us,
> Six are but three of us,
> Nine are but four of us,
> What can we possibly be?
> Would you know more of us?
> I'll tell you more of us.
> Twelve are but six of us,
> Five are but four, do you see?

ANS: Letters.

What creature walks in the morning on four feet, at noon upon two, at evening upon three?   *ANS: Man: as a baby on hands and knees, later on his feet, and in the evening of life with a cane. (This is, of course, the famous "Riddle of the Sphinx." The Sphinx [of Thebes] made a practice of proposing this riddle to all who happened to pass, and of killing all who failed to guess it. Nobdy guessed the riddle until Oedipus came along. Oedipus guessed the riddle, the Sphinx slew herself, and Oedipus became king of Thebes.)*

> Round as a biscuit, busy as a bee,
> Prettiest little thing you ever did see.

ANS: A watch.

> He went to the wood and caught it,
> He sate him downe and sought it;
> Because he could not find it,
> Home with him he brought it.

ANS: That is a thorne; for a man went to the wood, and caught a thorne in his foot, and then he sate him down, and sought to have pulled it out, and because he could not find it out, he must needs bring it home. (This riddle and its answer are quoted from "The Booke of Merry Riddles," published in England some time in the sixteenth century. The book became very popular and was apparently well known to Shakespeare, being mentioned in "The Merry Wives of Windsor," Act 1, Scene 1.)

> Ten fish I caught without an eye,
> And nine without a tail;
> Six had no head, and half of eight
> I weighed upon the scale.
> Now who can tell me as I ask it,
> How many fish were in my basket?

ANS: 0 (none). 10 without an I gives 0; nine without a tail gives 0, as does 6 without a head, etc.

Two legs sate upon three legs, and had one leg in her hand; then in came foure legs, and bare away one leg; then up start two legs, and threw three legs at foure legs, and brought againe one leg.   *ANS: That is a woman with two legs sate on a stoole with three legs, and had a leg of mutton in her hand; then came a dog that hath foure legs, and bare away the leg of mutton; then up start the woman, and threw the stoole with three legs at the dog with foure legs, and brought again the leg of mutton. (This riddle is also copied from "The Booke of Merry Riddles." It is the first riddle in the book, the one about the thorn being the second.)*

19

Letters, Words, and Numbers

RIDDLES ABOUT LETTERS

No Letter Named in Riddle

What letter is nine inches long?   *ANS: The letter Y; it is one-fourth of a yard.*

What letter is most useful to a deaf woman?   *ANS: The letter A, because it makes her hear.*

What letter made Queen Bess mind her P's and Q's? *ANS: The Armada (the R made her).*

What letter is never found in the alphabet?   *ANS: The one you mail.*

If all the letters in the alphabet were on a mountaintop, which letter would leave first?   *ANS: D would begin the descent.*

What letter of the alphabet is necessary to make a shoe? *ANS: The last.*

What letter will set one of the heavenly bodies in motion? *ANS: T, because it will make a star start.*

What letter travels the greatest distance?   *ANS: D, because it goes to the end of the world.*

What letter in the Dutch alphabet will name an English lady of title?   *ANS: A Dutch S.*

Which is the longest letter in the alphabet?   *ANS: An L.*
("Ell": A unit of length used chiefly in measuring cloth. In
England it is forty-five inches.)

If your mother-in-law were to fall overboard, what letter
would suit your wishes?   *ANS: Letter B.*

What one letter in the alphabet will spell the word potato?
ANS: The letter O; put them down one at a time until you
have put eight O's (potatoes).

Which are the poorest letters?   *ANS: The O's.*

What letters are most like a Roman emperor?   *ANS: The*
C's are.

What letters are in-visible, but never out of sight?   *ANS:*
I and S.

In the word CLOVES, why are C and S, although separated,
closely attached?   *ANS: Because there is LOVE between*
them.

Which two letters of the alphabet have nothing between
them?   *ANS: N and P; they have O between them.*

How would you express in two letters that you were twice
the bulk of your companion?   *ANS: I-W.*

What two letters express the most agreeable people in the
world?   *ANS: U and I.*

What two letters of the alphabet make a philosopher?
ANS: Y-Z (Y-Zed).

If you asked the alphabet to an afternoon party, which
letters could not come until later in the evening?   *ANS:*
The last six, because they cannot come until after T.

> A feeling all persons detest,
>   Although 'tis by everyone felt,
> By two letters fully expressed,
>   By twice two invariably spelt.

ANS: N-V (envy).

Which is the richest and which the poorest letter in the alphabet? *ANS: S and T, because we always hear of la richesse and la pauvreté.*

> Three letters three rivers proclaim;
> Three letters an ode give to fame;
> Three letters an attribute name;
> Three letters a compliment claim.

ANS: X,Y,D (Exe, Wye, Dee); L-E-G (elegy); N-R-G (energy); U-X-L (you excel).

What three letters make a man of a boy?   *ANS: A-G-E.*

Like what four letters of the alphabet is a honey-producing insect when in small health?   *ANS: Like A-B-C-D (a bee seedy).*

Why is a man who has studied and practiced the art of inlaying with variegated colors like four letters of the alphabet? *ANS: Because he's an N-M-L-R.*

How can you, with eight letters, tell a girl by the name of Ellen that she is everything that is delightful?   *ANS: U-R-A-B-U-T-L-N.*

When will there be but twenty-five letters in the alphabet? *ANS: When U and I are one.*

When does a blacksmith create a row in the alphabet? *ANS: When he makes A poke-R and shove-L.*

Why is a glass blower the most likely person to set one of the letters off at a gallop?   *ANS: Because he can make a D-canter.*

Why is the mark known as the cedilla in the French alphabet like a pearl?   *ANS: Because it is found at the bottom of the C.*

Why are the abbreviations of degrees tacked on to a man's name?   *ANS: To show that he is a man of letters.*

When were there only two vowels?   *ANS: In the days of No-A, before U and I were born.*

Why is an amiable and charming girl like one letter of the alphabet in deep thought, another on its way toward you, another bearing a torch, and another singing psalms? *ANS: Because she is A-musing, B-coming, D-lighting, and N-chanting.*

Letter Named in Riddle

Why should men avoid the letter A?   *ANS: Because it makes men mean.*

Why is the letter A like noon?   *ANS: Because it's the middle of day.*

Why is the letter A like honeysuckle?   *ANS: Because it always has a B following it.*

What must I do to the alphabet to remove A from it? *ANS: B-head it.*

Why are A, E, and U the handsome vowels?   *ANS: Because you can't have beauty without them.*

When did Chicago begin with a C and end with an E? *ANS: Chicago always began with C and END always began with E.*

When was B the first letter of the alphabet?   *ANS: In the days of No-A.*

When is a man like the letter B?   *ANS: When he's in bed.*

What comes after B in the alphabet?   *ANS: E.*

Why is the letter B like a hot fire?   *ANS: Because it makes oil boil.*

What does the letter B do for boys as they grow older? *ANS: It makes older boys bolder.*

Why is a teacher of girls like the letter C?   *ANS: She makes lasses into classes.*

Why is the letter C such a frigid letter?   *ANS: Because it's in the middle of ice and it makes old people cold people.*

Why is the letter D like a sailor?   *ANS: Because it follows the C.*

Why are the Dover cliffs like the letter D?   *ANS: Because they are next the sea.*

Why did Noah object to the letter D?   *ANS: Because it made the ark dark.*

Why is the letter D like a squalling child?   *ANS: Because it makes Ma mad.*

Why is the letter D like a wedding ring?   *ANS: Because we cannot be wed without it.*

Why is the letter D on horseback like an insult?   *ANS: Because it is D-riding.*

Why is the letter E like death?   *ANS: Because it is the end of life.*

Why is E the most unfortunate letter?   *ANS: Because it is never in cash, always in debt, and never out of danger.*

Why is the letter E gloomy and discontented?   *ANS: Because, though never out of health and pocket, it never appears in spirits.*

Why is the letter E like London?   *ANS: Because it is the capital of England.*

What ends with E, begins with P, and has a thousand letters? *ANS: Postoffice.*

Why is the final letter in EUROPE like a Parisian riot? *ANS: Because it's an E mute. ("Emeute": A seditious riot.)*

Why is the letter F like Paris?   *ANS: Because it is the capital of France.*

Why is the letter F like death?   *ANS: Because it makes all fall.*

Why is the letter F like a fishhook?   *ANS: Because it will make an eel feel.*

Why is the letter F like a cow's tail?   *ANS: Because it is the end of beef.*

Why is the letter G like the sun?   *ANS: Because it is the center of light.*

Why is the letter G like 12 P.M.?   *ANS: Because it is the middle of night.*

Why is a farmer astonished at the letter G?   *ANS: Because it converts oats into goats.*

Why was the reptile that stung Cleopatra like the letter H? *ANS: Because it was an asp-irate.*

Why is the letter I in the word CICERO like Arabia? *ANS: Because it is between two C's.*

Why is I the luckiest of the vowels?   *ANS: Because it is in the center of bliss, while E is in hell, and all the others are in purgatory.*

Why did Kaiser Wilhelm spell culture with a K?   *ANS: Because the Allies had command of the seas.*

Why is the letter K like a pig's tail?   *ANS: Because it is the end of pork.*

Why is the letter L like reforming a sweetheart?   *ANS: Because it makes over a lover.*

Why should a housewife never put the letter M into her refrigerator?   *ANS: Because it will change ice into mice.*

Why is the letter N like a pig?   *ANS: Because it makes a sty nasty.*

Why is the letter N like summer?   *ANS: Because it makes ice nice.*

Why is the letter N like a buck's tail?   *ANS: Because it is the end of venison.*

Why is the letter O like a neatly kept house?   *ANS: Because it is always in order.*

Why is a horse like the letter O?   *ANS: Because "gee" makes it go.*

Why is O the only vowel that is sounded?   *ANS: Because all the others are in audible.*

Why are the fourteenth and fifteenth letters of the alphabet of more importance that the others?   *ANS: Because we cannot get on without them.*

Why should a stupid fellow who is about to take an examination study the letter P?   *ANS: Because it can make an ass pass.*

Why is a false friend like the letter P?   *ANS: Because, although first in pity, he is always last in help.*

Why is the letter P like a Roman emperor?   *ANS: Because it is near O.*

Why is the letter R indispensable to friendship?   *ANS: Because without it friends would be fiends.*

Why is the letter R so profitable?   *ANS: Because it makes ice into rice.*

Why is kiss spelled with two S's?   *ANS: Because it always takes two to complete the spell.*

How do we know that S is a scary letter?   *ANS: It makes cream scream.*

Why is a sewing machine like the letter S?   *ANS: Because it makes common needles needless.*

Why is the letter S like thunder?   *ANS: Because it makes our milk sour milk.*

Why is T the happiest letter of the alphabet?   *ANS: Because it is next to U.*

Tommy Tucker took two strings and tied two turtles to two tall trees. How many T's in that?   *ANS: There are two T's in that.*

Why is the letter T like Easter?   *ANS: Because it is the last of Lent.*

What starts with T, ends with T, and is full of tea?   *ANS: Teapot.*

Why is the letter T like matrimony?   *ANS: Because it is the end of quiet and the beginning of trouble.*

Why is an island like the letter T?   *ANS: Because it is in the middle of water.*

Why are two T's like hops?   *ANS: Because they make beer better.*

Why is the letter T like an amphibious animal?   *ANS: Because it lives both in earth and in water.*

Why is the Isthmus of Suez like the first U in cucumber? *ANS: Because it is between two seas.*

Why is U the jolliest letter?   *ANS: Because it is always in the midst of fun.*

Why is the nose on your face like the V in civility?   *ANS: Because it is between two eyes.*

Why is scandal like the letter W?   *ANS: Because it makes ill will.*

Why is the letter W like a maid of honor?   *ANS: Because it is always in waiting.*

Why is the letter X like a pensive widow? *ANS: Because it is never in consolable.*

Why is the letter Y like a spendthrift youth? *ANS: Because it makes Pa pay.*

Why should a boy avoid the letter Y? *ANS: Because it can turn a lad into a lady.*

RIDDLES ABOUT WORDS

The Spelling of Words

Which is easier to spell—fiddle-dee-dee or fiddle-dee-dum? *ANS: The former is spelled with more E's.*

Why is it that I cannot spell CUPID? *ANS: Because when I get to C-U, I forget everything else.*

When can donkey be spelled with one letter? *ANS: When it's U.*

Spell BRANDY in three letters. *ANS: B, R, and Y.*

Spell butter in four letters. *ANS: G-O-A-T.*

Spell auburn locks in two letters. *ANS: S and Y.*

Spell mousetrap in three letters. *ANS: C-A-T.*

Spell dried grass in three letters. *ANS: H-A-Y.*

Spell hard water in three letters. *ANS: I-C-E.*

Spell black water in three letters. *ANS: I-N-K.*

Spell donkey in three letters. *ANS: Y-O-U.*

How do you spell blind pig? *ANS: B-L-N-D P-G. You have to spell it that way because a blind pig has no eyes.*

How, besides NME, can you spell enemy in three letters? *ANS: F-O-E.*

Nebuchadnezzar, king of the Jews, sat in the corner to put on his shoes. Can you spell that with four letters?   *ANS: Yes, T-H-A-T.*

Railroad crossing, look out for the cars!
Can you spell that without any R's?
ANS: Yes, T-H-A-T.

England, Ireland, Scotland, Wales,
Monkeys, rats, and wiggle-tails.
Spell that with four letters.   *ANS: T-H-A-T.*

What Word?

What word when deprived of a letter makes you sick?
ANS: Music.

What word is nearly always pronounced wrong, even by the best scholars?   *ANS: The word WRONG.*

What word of five letters has six left after you take two away?   *ANS: Sixty.*

What is the longest word in the English language?   *ANS: SMILES, because it has a mile between the first and last letters.*

From a word of five letters take two and leave one.   *ANS: Alone less A-L gives one.*

What is a word of fifteen letters from which you can subtract twelve and leave ten?   *ANS: Pretentiousness.*

Take two letters from a five-letter word and have one left.
ANS: Stone—one.

What word of eight letters is there from which you can subtract five and leave ten?   *ANS: Tendency.*

What words can be prounced quicker and shorter by adding a syllable to them?   *ANS: Quick and short.*

What word of four letters still has five left when three of the letters are taken away? *ANS: Love. From this word take away L, O, and E, leaving V, the Roman number five.*

Take two letters away from a four-letter word and have four left. *ANS: From FIVE take F and E, leaving IV (four).*

What single word would you put down to indicate forty dollars borrowed from you? *ANS: XL lent.*

How do you pronounce V-O-L-I-X? *ANS: Volume nine.*

What is the longest sentence in the world? *ANS: "Go to prison for life."*

What is the favorite word with women? *ANS: The last one.*

How would you express in one word having encountered a doctor of medicine? *ANS: Metaphysician.*

At a dancing party, what single word would call the musicians to their posts, and at the same time tell the hour to begin dancing? *ANS: Attendance (at ten dance).*

> A word there is five syllables contains;
> Take one away—not one of them remains.

ANS: Monosyllable. Take away MO and leave NO SYLLABLE.

What is that which has a name of three letters but still has its name when two of the letters are taken away? *ANS: Tea, or Bee.*

Make one word from the letters of NEW DOOR. *ANS: ONE WORD.*

Make just one word from these letters: D-E-J-N-O-O-R-S-T-U-W. *ANS: JUST ONE WORD.*

Make one word from nine thumps. *ANS: PUNISHMENT.*

There is a six-letter word of which La is the middle, is the beginning, and the ending. What is the word? *ANS: Island.*

In a certain word ST is in the middle, in the beginning, and the ending. What is the word? *ANS: Inkstand.*

What is the difference between a fort and a fortress? *ANS: The latter is harder to silence.*

What is the difference between here and there? *ANS: The letter T.*

RIDDLES ABOUT NUMBERS

What odd number when beheaded becomes even? *ANS: Seven (S-even).*

From what number can you take half and leave nothing? *ANS: 8.*

When a lady faints, what number will restore her? *ANS: You must bring her 2.*

Which is greater, six dozen dozen or half a dozen dozen? *ANS: Six dozen dozen; it is 864, while the other is 72.*

When do 2 and 2 make more than 4? *ANS: When they make 22.*

Why is twice ten like twice eleven? *ANS: Because twice ten is twenty, and twice eleven is twenty-two (twenty, too).*

How many times may 19 be subtracted from 189? *ANS: Only once; any subsequent subtraction must be from a smaller number.*

Why should the number 288 never be spoken in refined company? *ANS: Because it is two gross.*

Why is a figure 9 like a peacock?   *ANS: Because it is nothing (0) without its tail.*

If two is company and three is a crowd, what are four and five?   *ANS: Nine.*

> My number, definite and known,
>> Is ten times ten, told ten times o'er;
> Though half of me is one alone,
>> And half exceeds all count and score.

ANS: Thousand (thou-sand).

If I dig a hole two feet square and two feet deep, how much dirt is in the hole?   *ANS: None.*

What is the difference between 100 and 1000?   *ANS: Naught.*

Take ten from nine and leave only yourself.   *ANS: From IX take X, leaving I.*

> By equal division I know I am right;
> The half of thirteen you'll find to be eight.

ANS: Divide XIII in halves by a horizontal line and get VIII.

Make five less by adding to it.   *ANS: I to V and get IV.*

Behead forty and leave fifty.   *ANS: Take X from XL and leave L.*

From nineteen take one and leave twenty.   *ANS: From XIX take I and leave XX.*

What would you add to nine to make six?   *ANS: S; IX plus S makes SIX.*

Show that two-thirds of six is nine.   *ANS: Two-thirds of SIX is IX, nine.*

20

What Is the Difference?

What is the difference between an apple and a pretty girl? *ANS: One you have to squeeze to get cider, the other you have to get 'side her to squeeze.*

What is the difference between an auction and seasickness? *ANS: One is a sale of effects, the other effects of a sail.*

What is the difference between a barber and the mother of several children?   *ANS: One has razors to shave, the other has shavers to raise.*

What is the difference between a bare head and a hair bed? *ANS: One flees for shelter, the other is shelter for fleas.*

What is the difference between a beached vessel and a wrecked airplane?   *ANS: One grounds on the land, the other lands on the ground.*

What is the difference between a blacksmith and a safe steed? *ANS: One is a horseshoer, the other is a sure horse.*

What is the difference between the rear light of an automobile and a book of fiction?   *ANS: One is a taillight, the other is a light tale.*

What is the difference between a bouquet of flowers and a bottle of whisky?   *ANS: One makes a nosegay, the other makes a gay nose.*

What is the difference between a butcher and a fashionable young woman?   *ANS: One kills to dress, the other dresses to kill.*

What is the difference between your dividing your hair in the dark through not having time to wait for candles, and a man's running in debt to send his visitors away contented? *ANS: The former is the parting guessed, owing to speed; the latter is owing, to speed the parting guest.*

What is the difference between a volcano and a butterfly? *ANS: In one the lava comes out of the crater, in the other the cratur comes out of the larva.*

What is the difference between a cashier and a schoolmaster? *ANS: One minds the till, the other tills the mind.*

What is the difference between a chess player and a habitual toper?   *ANS: One watches the pawn, the other pawns the watch.*

What is the difference between a chicken that cannot hold its head up, and seven days?   *ANS: The first is a weak one, the other is one week.*

What is the difference between a china shop and a furniture store?   *ANS: One sells tea sets, the other sells settees.*

What is the difference between a choirmaster and a lady's dress?   *ANS: One trains a choir, the other acquires a train.*

What is the difference between a crown prince and the water in a fountain?   *ANS: One is heir to the throne, the other is thrown to the air.*

What is the difference between a dog losing his hair, and a man painting a small building?   *ANS: One sheds his coat, the other coats his shed.*

What is the difference between a donkey and a postage stamp?   *ANS: One you lick with a stick, the other you stick with a lick.*

What is the difference between an editor and his wife? *ANS: One writes articles to set, the other sets articles to right.*

What is the difference between an elephant and a flea? *ANS: An elephant can have fleas, but a flea cannot have elephants.*

What is the difference between an emperor and a barefoot beggar?   *ANS: One issues manifestoes, the other manifests toes without his shoes.*

What is the difference between a locomotive engineer and a schoolmaster?   *ANS: One minds the train, the other trains the mind.*

What is the difference between a farmer guiding a plow and a steamship in mid-ocean?   *ANS: One sees the plow, the other plows the sea.*

What is the difference between a farmer and a seamstress? *ANS: One gathers what he sows, the other sews what she gathers.*

What is the difference between a fish dinner and a racing establishment?   *ANS: At one a man finds sauces for his table, at the other he finds a stable for his horses.*

What is the difference between a good soldier and a fashionable young lady?   *ANS: One faces the powder, the other powders the face.*

What is the difference between honey and a black eye? *ANS: One comes from a laboring bee, the other from a belaboring.*

What is the difference between a horse who, being entered for a race, is withdrawn, and one who starts in the race and is beaten?   *ANS: One fails to start, the other starts to fail.*

What is the difference between an Indian and an Irishman? *ANS: One smokes a pipe of peace, the other smokes a piece of pipe.*

What is the difference between an Irishman frozen to death, and a Highlander on a mountain peak in January?   *ANS: One is kilt with the cold, the other is cold with the kilt.*

What is the difference between the ancient Israelites and an old-fashioned washstand? *ANS: The former had hewers of wood and drawers of water, the latter have ewers of water and drawers of wood.*

What is the difference between killed soldiers and repaired garments? *ANS: The former are dead men, the latter are mended.*

What is the difference between Kossuth and a half-starved countryman? *ANS: One was a native of Hungary, the other is a hungry native.*

What is the difference between the liqueur called "gold-water" and a conservatory door that won't close? *ANS: One is a glass of acqua d'oro, the other is an awkward door o' glass.*

What is the difference between a man struck with amazement, and the tail of a Dalmatian dog? *ANS: One is rooted to the spot, the other is spotted to the root.*

What is the difference between the last riddle and your aunt who squints? *ANS: One is a query with an answer, the other an aunt, sir, with a queer eye.*

What is the difference between a man dodging footwear that is thrown at him, and a man chasing a flock of ducks out of his pond? *ANS: One ducks the shoes, the other shoos the ducks.*

What is the difference between a nurse taking a patient's pulse, and a champion runner? *ANS: One records the beats, the other beats the records.*

What is the difference between an oak tree and a tight shoe? *ANS: One makes acorns, the other makes corns ache.*

What is the difference between an organist and a cold in the head? *ANS: One knows the stops, the other stops the nose.*

What is the difference between a person late for a train, and a teacher in a girls' school?   *ANS: One misses the train, the other trains the misses.*

What is the difference between a pitcher of water, and a man throwing his wife off a bridge?   *ANS: One is water in the pitcher, the other is pitch her in the water.*

What is the difference between a pugilist and a man with a cold?   *ANS: One knows his blows, the other blows his nose.*

What is the difference between a professional pianist giving a concert, and a member of his audience?   *ANS: One plays for his pay, the other pays for his play.*

What is the difference between a pugilist and a lapdog?   *ANS: One faces the licks, the other licks the face.*

What is the difference between a real-estate agent and the latest thing in cravats?   *ANS: One is agent for property, the other a proper tie for a gent.*

What is the difference between a rejected lover and an accepted one?   *ANS: The former misses the kiss, the latter kisses the miss.*

What is the difference between a rifleman firing wide of his target, and a man who blacks his wife's eyes?   *ANS: One misses his mark, the other marks his missus.*

What is the difference between a skilled marksman and the man who tends the targets?   *ANS: One hits the mark, the other marks the hits.*

What is the difference between stabbing a man and killing a hog?   *ANS: One is assault with intent to kill, the other is killing with intent to salt.*

What is the difference between a chimney sweep and a man in mourning?   *ANS: One is blacked with soot, the other is suited with black.*

What is the difference between a tailor and a groom? *ANS: One mends a tear, the other tends a mare.*

What is the difference between a skillful miner and a wealthy toper? *ANS: One turns his quartz into gold, the other turns his gold into quarts.*

What is the difference between a winter storm and a child with a cold? *ANS: In the one it snows, it blows; the other blows its nose.*

What is the difference between a woman and a postage stamp? *ANS: One is female, the other is mail fee.*

What is the difference between a certain part of Africa, and the shade of Hamlet's father stalking in winter? *ANS: One is the Gold Coast, the other is a cold ghost.*

What is the difference between a crazy hare and a counterfeit coin? *ANS: One is a mad bunny, the other is bad money.*

What is the difference between a fisherman and a lazy schoolboy? *ANS: One baits his hook, the other hates his book.*

What is the difference between a girl and a nightcap? *ANS: One is born to wed, the other is worn to bed.*

What is the difference between a light in a cave and a dance in an inn? *ANS: One is a taper in a cavern, the other is a caper in a tavern.*

What is the difference between your last will and testament, and a man who has just eaten as much as he can? *ANS: One is signed and dated, the other is dined and sated.*

What is the difference between a photographer and the measles? *ANS: One makes facsimiles, the other makes sick families.*

What is the difference between an empty tube and a foolish Dutchman? *ANS: One is a hollow cylinder, the other is a silly Hollander.*

What is the difference between an undersized witch and a deer trying to escape from a hunter?   *ANS: One is a stunted hag, the other is a hunted stag.*

What is the difference between a thief and a church bell? *ANS: One steals from the people, the other peals from the steeple.*

What is the difference between a cloud and a whipped child?   *ANS: One pours with rain, the other roars with pain.*

What is the difference between a sewing machine and a kiss? *ANS: One sews seams nice, the other seems so nice.*

What is the difference between a jeweler and a jailer? *ANS: One sells watches, the other watches cells.*

What is the difference between a beautiful girl and a mouse? *ANS: One charms the he's, the other harms the cheese.*

What is the difference between a cat and a comma?   *ANS: One has its claws at the end of its paws, the other its pause at the end of its clause.*

What is the difference between a chatterbox and a mirror? *ANS: One talks without reflecting, the other reflects without talking.*

What is the difference between a man going upstairs and a man looking upstairs?   *ANS: One is stepping up the stairs, the other is staring up the steps.*

What is the difference between a glutton and a hungry man? *ANS: One eats too long, the other longs to eat.*

What is the difference between a retired sailor and a blind man?   *ANS: One cannot go to sea, the other cannot see to go.*

What is the difference between a pianist and sixteen ounces of lead?   *ANS: One pounds away, the other weighs a pound.*

What is the difference between a moneyless man and a feather bed? *ANS: One is hard up, the other is soft down.*

What is the difference between a hill and a pill? *ANS: One is hard to get up, the other is hard to get down.*

What is the difference between an elevator and the man who runs it? *ANS: One is lowered to take passengers up, the other is hired to do it.*

What is the difference between a correspondent and a co-respondent? *ANS: One is a man who does write, the other is a man who does wrong.*

What is the difference between a professor of natation and a Turk, the inhabitants of whose harem are getting thinner? *ANS: One watches his swimmin' lesson with pleasure, the other watches his women lessen with pain.*

What is the difference between a bright scholar and a boot-black? *ANS: One shines at the head, the other at the foot.*

What is the difference between a summer dress in winter, and an extracted tooth? *ANS: One is too thin, the other is tooth out.*

What is the difference between a man taking an oath of office, and a suit of castoff clothes? *ANS: One is sworn in, the other is worn out.*

What is the difference between forms and ceremonies? *ANS: You sit upon one and stand on the other. ("Form": A long seat; a bench; as, a school form.)*

Why were the governments of Algiers and Malta as different as light and darkness? *ANS: Because one was governed by deys, the other by knights.*

What is the difference between a sailor and the manager of a theater? *ANS: One likes to see a lighthouse, the other doesn't.*

What is the difference between an old barn and a bad boy?
ANS: One needs shingling on top, the other on the bottom.

What is the difference between a cat and a match?   *ANS:
One lights on its feet, the other lights on its head.*

What is the difference between an ear trumpet and a tunnel?
ANS: One gets hollered in, the other gets hollowed out.

What is the difference between the treatment of a child by
its mother and by a doctor?   *ANS: The mother whacks
and loves it, the doctor vaccinates it.*

What is the difference between a clock and a partnership?
*ANS: When a watch is wound up it goes; when the partner-
ship is wound up it stops.*

What is the difference between a fish and the husband of a
vixen?   *ANS: One lives in cold water, the other in hot.*

What is the difference between the earth and the sea?
ANS: One is dirty, the other is tide-y.

What is the difference between a carriage wheel and a
carriage horse?   *ANS: One goes better when it is tired,
the other doesn't.*

What is the difference between a bell and an organ?   *ANS:
One rings when it is tolled, the other will be blowed first.*

What is the difference between Noah's ark and an arch-
bishop?   *ANS: One was a high ark, the other is a hierarch.*

What is the difference between reckless speculation and a
slice of bacon?   *ANS: One is a rash thing, the other is a
rasher.*

What is the difference between horse racing and going to
church?   *ANS: One makes men bet, the other makes them
better.*

What is the difference between a dinner bell and a cook?
ANS: One makes a din, the other a dinner.

What is the difference between a sailor and a soldier?
ANS: One tars his ropes, the other pitches his tent.

What is the difference between a physician and a magician?
ANS: One is a cupper, the other is a sorcerer.

What is the difference between a cow and a rickety chair?
ANS: One gives milk, the other gives way.

What is the difference between a baby and a shipwrecked sailor? *ANS: One clings to his ma, the other clings to his spar.*

What is the difference between Oliver Cromwell and Queen Elizabeth? *ANS: The former was a wonder, but the latter was a Tudor.*

What is the difference between a well-dressed man and a tired dog? *ANS: The man wears an entire suit, the dog just pants.*

What is the difference between a dog's tail and a rich man?
ANS: One keeps a-waggin', the other keeps a carriage.

What is the difference between a beehive and a bad potato?
ANS: One is a bee-holder, the other a specked 'tater.

What is the difference between a cat and a bullfrog?
ANS: The cat has nine lives, but the bullfrog croaks every night.

What is the difference between the manner of death of a barber and that of a sculptor? *ANS: The barber curls up and dyes, while the sculptor makes faces and busts.*

What is the difference between a young girl and an old hat?
ANS: One has feeling, the other has felt.

What is the difference between a bee and a donkey? *ANS: One gets all the honey, the other gets all the whacks.*

What is the difference between an honest laundress and a dishonest one? *ANS: One irons your linen, the other steals it.*

What is the difference between a fixed star and a meteor? *ANS: One is a sun, the other a darter.*

What is the difference between a ballet dancer and a duck? *ANS: One goes quick on her beautiful legs, the other goes quack on her beautiful eggs.*

What is the difference between a king's son, a monkey's mother, a bald head, and an orphan?   *ANS: The king's son is the heir apparent, a monkey's mother is a hairy parent, a bald head has no hair apparent, and an orphan has nary a parent.*

What is the difference between a doe, an overpriced article, and a donkey?   *ANS: A doe is a deer, an overpriced article is too dear, and a donkey is you, dear.*

What is the difference between Noah's ark and Joan of Arc? *ANS: One was made of wood, the other was Maid of Orleans.*

What is the difference between a man with an unnatural voice and one with unnatural teeth?   *ANS: One has a falsetto voice, the other a false set o' teeth.*

What is the difference between a very old woman and a cow?   *ANS: One lives in the past, the other in the pasture.*

Why is this riddle the last in the book?   *ANS: Because there's none after it.*

A CATALOGUE OF SELECTED DOVER BOOKS
IN ALL FIELDS OF INTEREST

A CATALOGUE OF SELECTED DOVER BOOKS
IN ALL FIELDS OF INTEREST

WHAT IS SCIENCE?, *N. Campbell*
The role of experiment and measurement, the function of mathematics, the nature of scientific laws, the difference between laws and theories, the limitations of science, and many similarly provocative topics are treated clearly and without technicalities by an eminent scientist. "Still an excellent introduction to scientific philosophy," H. Margenau in *Physics Today*. "A first-rate primer . . . deserves a wide audience," *Scientific American*. 192pp. 5⅜ x 8.
60043-2 Paperbound $1.25

THE NATURE OF LIGHT AND COLOUR IN THE OPEN AIR, *M. Minnaert*
Why are shadows sometimes blue, sometimes green, or other colors depending on the light and surroundings? What causes mirages? Why do multiple suns and moons appear in the sky? Professor Minnaert explains these unusual phenomena and hundreds of others in simple, easy-to-understand terms based on optical laws and the properties of light and color. No mathematics is required but artists, scientists, students, and everyone fascinated by these "tricks" of nature will find thousands of useful and amazing pieces of information. Hundreds of observational experiments are suggested which require no special equipment. 200 illustrations; 42 photos. xvi + 362pp. 5⅜ x 8.
20196-1 Paperbound $2.00

THE STRANGE STORY OF THE QUANTUM, AN ACCOUNT FOR THE GENERAL READER OF THE GROWTH OF IDEAS UNDERLYING OUR PRESENT ATOMIC KNOWLEDGE, *B. Hoffmann*
Presents lucidly and expertly, with barest amount of mathematics, the problems and theories which led to modern quantum physics. Dr. Hoffmann begins with the closing years of the 19th century, when certain trifling discrepancies were noticed, and with illuminating analogies and examples takes you through the brilliant concepts of Planck, Einstein, Pauli, Broglie, Bohr, Schroedinger, Heisenberg, Dirac, Sommerfeld, Feynman, etc. This edition includes a new, long postscript carrying the story through 1958. "Of the books attempting an account of the history and contents of our modern atomic physics which have come to my attention, this is the best," H. Margenau, Yale University, in *American Journal of Physics*. 32 tables and line illustrations. Index. 275pp. 5⅜ x 8.
20518-5 Paperbound $2.00

GREAT IDEAS OF MODERN MATHEMATICS: THEIR NATURE AND USE, *Jagjit Singh*
Reader with only high school math will understand main mathematical ideas of modern physics, astronomy, genetics, psychology, evolution, etc. better than many who use them as tools, but comprehend little of their basic structure. Author uses his wide knowledge of non-mathematical fields in brilliant exposition of differential equations, matrices, group theory, logic, statistics, problems of mathematical foundations, imaginary numbers, vectors, etc. Original publication. 2 appendixes. 2 indexes. 65 ills. 322pp. 5⅜ x 8.
20587-8 Paperbound $2.25

THE MUSIC OF THE SPHERES: THE MATERIAL UNIVERSE — FROM ATOM TO QUASAR, SIMPLY EXPLAINED, *Guy Murchie*
Vast compendium of fact, modern concept and theory, observed and calculated data, historical background guides intelligent layman through the material universe. Brilliant exposition of earth's construction, explanations for moon's craters, atmospheric components of Venus and Mars (with data from recent fly-by's), sun spots, sequences of star birth and death, neighboring galaxies, contributions of Galileo, Tycho Brahe, Kepler, etc.; and (Vol. 2) construction of the atom (describing newly discovered sigma and xi subatomic particles), theories of sound, color and light, space and time, including relativity theory, quantum theory, wave theory, probability theory, work of Newton, Maxwell, Faraday, Einstein, de Broglie, etc. "Best presentation yet offered to the intelligent general reader," *Saturday Review*. Revised (1967). Index. 319 illustrations by the author. Total of xx + 644pp. 5⅜ x 8½.
21809-0, 21810-4   Two volume set, paperbound $5.00

FOUR LECTURES ON RELATIVITY AND SPACE, *Charles Proteus Steinmetz*
Lecture series, given by great mathematician and electrical engineer, generally considered one of the best popular-level expositions of special and general relativity theories and related questions. Steinmetz translates complex mathematical reasoning into language accessible to laymen through analogy, example and comparison. Among topics covered are relativity of motion, location, time; of mass; acceleration; 4-dimensional time-space; geometry of the gravitational field; curvature and bending of space; non-Euclidean geometry. Index. 40 illustrations. x + 142pp. 5⅜ x 8½.   61771-8 Paperbound $1.35

HOW TO KNOW THE WILD FLOWERS, *Mrs. William Starr Dana*
Classic nature book that has introduced thousands to wonders of American wild flowers. Color-season principle of organization is easy to use, even by those with no botanical training, and the genial, refreshing discussions of history, folklore, uses of over 1,000 native and escape flowers, foliage plants are informative as well as fun to read. Over 170 full-page plates, collected from several editions, may be colored in to make permanent records of finds. Revised to conform with 1950 edition of Gray's Manual of Botany. xlii + 438pp. 5⅜ x 8½.   20332-8 Paperbound $2.50

MANUAL OF THE TREES OF NORTH AMERICA, *Charles Sprague Sargent*
Still unsurpassed as most comprehensive, reliable study of North American tree characteristics, precise locations and distribution. By dean of American dendrologists. Every tree native to U.S., Canada, Alaska; 185 genera, 717 species, described in detail—leaves, flowers, fruit, winterbuds, bark, wood, growth habits, etc. plus discussion of varieties and local variants, immaturity variations. Over 100 keys, including unusual 11-page analytical key to genera, aid in identification. 783 clear illustrations of flowers, fruit, leaves. An unmatched permanent reference work for all nature lovers. Second enlarged (1926) edition. Synopsis of families. Analytical key to genera. Glossary of technical terms. Index. 783 illustrations, 1 map. Total of 982pp. 5⅜ x 8.
20277-1, 20278-X Two volume set, paperbound $6.00

IT'S FUN TO MAKE THINGS FROM SCRAP MATERIALS,
Evelyn Glantz Hershoff
What use are empty spools, tin cans, bottle tops? What can be made from rubber bands, clothes pins, paper clips, and buttons? This book provides simply worded instructions and large diagrams showing you how to make cookie cutters, toy trucks, paper turkeys, Halloween masks, telephone sets, aprons, linoleum block- and spatter prints — in all 399 projects! Many are easy enough for young children to figure out for themselves; some challenging enough to entertain adults; all are remarkably ingenious ways to make things from materials that cost pennies or less! Formerly "Scrap Fun for Everyone." Index. 214 illustrations. 373pp. 5⅜ x 8½.   21251-3 Paperbound $1.75

SYMBOLIC LOGIC and THE GAME OF LOGIC, *Lewis Carroll*
"Symbolic Logic" is not concerned with modern symbolic logic, but is instead a collection of over 380 problems posed with charm and imagination, using the syllogism and a fascinating diagrammatic method of drawing conclusions. In "The Game of Logic" Carroll's whimsical imagination devises a logical game played with 2 diagrams and counters (included) to manipulate hundreds of tricky syllogisms. The final section, "Hit or Miss" is a lagniappe of 101 additional puzzles in the delightful Carroll manner. Until this reprint edition, both of these books were rarities costing up to $15 each. Symbolic Logic: Index. xxxi + 199pp. The Game of Logic: 96pp. 2 vols. bound as one. 5⅜ x 8.
20492-8 Paperbound $2.50

MATHEMATICAL PUZZLES OF SAM LOYD, PART I
selected and edited by M. Gardner
Choice puzzles by the greatest American puzzle creator and innovator. Selected from his famous collection, "Cyclopedia of Puzzles," they retain the unique style and historical flavor of the originals. There are posers based on arithmetic, algebra, probability, game theory, route tracing, topology, counter and sliding block, operations research, geometrical dissection. Includes the famous "14-15" puzzle which was a national craze, and his "Horse of a Different Color" which sold millions of copies. 117 of his most ingenious puzzles in all. 120 line drawings and diagrams. Solutions. Selected references. xx + 167pp. 5⅜ x 8.
20498-7 Paperbound $1.35

STRING FIGURES AND HOW TO MAKE THEM, *Caroline Furness Jayne*
107 string figures plus variations selected from the best primitive and modern examples developed by Navajo, Apache, pygmies of Africa, Eskimo, in Europe, Australia, China, etc. The most readily understandable, easy-to-follow book in English on perennially popular recreation. Crystal-clear exposition; step-by-step diagrams. Everyone from kindergarten children to adults looking for unusual diversion will be endlessly amused. Index. Bibliography. Introduction by A. C. Haddon. 17 full-page plates, 960 illustrations. xxiii + 401pp. 5⅜ x 8½.
20152-X Paperbound $2.25

PAPER FOLDING FOR BEGINNERS, *W. D. Murray and F. J. Rigney*
A delightful introduction to the varied and entertaining Japanese art of origami (paper folding), with a full, crystal-clear text that anticipates every difficulty; over 275 clearly labeled diagrams of all important stages in creation. You get results at each stage, since complex figures are logically developed from simpler ones. 43 different pieces are explained: sailboats, frogs, roosters, etc. 6 photographic plates. 279 diagrams. 95pp. 5⅝ x 8⅜.
20713-7 Paperbound $1.00

PRINCIPLES OF ART HISTORY,
H. Wölfflin

Analyzing such terms as "baroque," "classic," "neoclassic," "primitive," "picturesque," and 164 different works by artists like Botticelli, van Cleve, Dürer, Hobbema, Holbein, Hals, Rembrandt, Titian, Brueghel, Vermeer, and many others, the author establishes the classifications of art history and style on a firm, concrete basis. This classic of art criticism shows what really occurred between the 14th-century primitives and the sophistication of the 18th century in terms of basic attitudes and philosophies. "A remarkable lesson in the art of seeing," Sat. Rev. of Literature. Translated from the 7th German edition. 150 illustrations. 254pp. 6⅛ x 9¼. 20276-3 Paperbound $2.25

PRIMITIVE ART,
Franz Boas

This authoritative and exhaustive work by a great American anthropologist covers the entire gamut of primitive art. Pottery, leatherwork, metal work, stone work, wood, basketry, are treated in detail. Theories of primitive art, historical depth in art history, technical virtuosity, unconscious levels of patterning, symbolism, styles, literature, music, dance, etc. A must book for the interested layman, the anthropologist, artist, handicrafter (hundreds of unusual motifs), and the historian. Over 900 illustrations (50 ceramic vessels, 12 totem poles, etc.). 376pp. 5⅜ x 8. 20025-6 Paperbound $2.50

THE GENTLEMAN AND CABINET MAKER'S DIRECTOR,
Thomas Chippendale

A reprint of the 1762 catalogue of furniture designs that went on to influence generations of English and Colonial and Early Republic American furniture makers. The 200 plates, most of them full-page sized, show Chippendale's designs for French (Louis XV), Gothic, and Chinese-manner chairs, sofas, canopy and dome beds, cornices, chamber organs, cabinets, shaving tables, commodes, picture frames, frets, candle stands, chimney pieces, decorations, etc. The drawings are all elegant and highly detailed; many include construction diagrams and elevations. A supplement of 24 photographs shows surviving pieces of original and Chippendale-style pieces of furniture. Brief biography of Chippendale by N. I. Bienenstock, editor of Furniture World. Reproduced from the 1762 edition. 200 plates, plus 19 photographic plates. vi + 249pp. 9⅛ x 12¼. 21601-2 Paperbound $3.50

AMERICAN ANTIQUE FURNITURE: A BOOK FOR AMATEURS,
Edgar G. Miller, Jr.

Standard introduction and practical guide to identification of valuable American antique furniture. 2115 illustrations, mostly photographs taken by the author in 148 private homes, are arranged in chronological order in extensive chapters on chairs, sofas, chests, desks, bedsteads, mirrors, tables, clocks, and other articles. Focus is on furniture accessible to the collector, including simpler pieces and a larger than usual coverage of Empire style. Introductory chapters identify structural elements, characteristics of various styles, how to avoid fakes, etc. "We are frequently asked to name some book on American furniture that will meet the requirements of the novice collector, the beginning dealer, and . . . the general public. . . . We believe Mr. Miller's two volumes more completely satisfy this specification than any other work," Antiques. Appendix. Index. Total of vi + 1106pp. 7⅞ x 10¾. 21599-7, 21600-4 Two volume set, paperbound $7.50

THE BAD CHILD'S BOOK OF BEASTS, MORE BEASTS FOR WORSE CHILDREN, and A MORAL ALPHABET, *H. Belloc*
Hardly and anthology of humorous verse has appeared in the last 50 years without at least a couple of these famous nonsense verses. But one must see the entire volumes — with all the delightful original illustrations by Sir Basil Blackwood — to appreciate fully Belloc's charming and witty verses that play so subacidly on the platitudes of life and morals that beset his day — and ours. A great humor classic. Three books in one. Total of 157pp. 5⅜ x 8.
20749-8 Paperbound $1.00

THE DEVIL'S DICTIONARY, *Ambrose Bierce*
Sardonic and irreverent barbs puncturing the pomposities and absurdities of American politics, business, religion, literature, and arts, by the country's greatest satirist in the classic tradition. Epigrammatic as Shaw, piercing as Swift, American as Mark Twain, Will Rogers, and Fred Allen, Bierce will always remain the favorite of a small coterie of enthusiasts, and of writers and speakers whom he supplies with "some of the most gorgeous witticisms of the English language" (H. L. Mencken). Over 1000 entries in alphabetical order. 144pp. 5⅜ x 8.
20487-1 Paperbound $1.00

THE COMPLETE NONSENSE OF EDWARD LEAR.
This is the only complete edition of this master of gentle madness available at a popular price. *A Book of Nonsense, Nonsense Songs, More Nonsense Songs and Stories* in their entirety with all the old favorites that have delighted children and adults for years. The Dong With A Luminous Nose, The Jumblies, The Owl and the Pussycat, and hundreds of other bits of wonderful nonsense. 214 limericks, 3 sets of Nonsense Botany, 5 Nonsense Alphabets, 546 drawings by Lear himself, and much more. 320pp. 5⅜ x 8. 20167-8 Paperbound $1.75

THE WIT AND HUMOR OF OSCAR WILDE, *ed. by Alvin Redman*
Wilde at his most brilliant, in 1000 epigrams exposing weaknesses and hypocrisies of "civilized" society. Divided into 49 categories—sin, wealth, women, America, etc.—to aid writers, speakers. Includes excerpts from his trials, books, plays, criticism. Formerly "The Epigrams of Oscar Wilde." Introduction by Vyvyan Holland, Wilde's only living son. Introductory essay by editor. 260pp. 5⅜ x 8.
20602-5 Paperbound $1.50

A CHILD'S PRIMER OF NATURAL HISTORY, *Oliver Herford*
Scarcely an anthology of whimsy and humor has appeared in the last 50 years without a contribution from Oliver Herford. Yet the works from which these examples are drawn have been almost impossible to obtain! Here at last are Herford's improbable definitions of a menagerie of familiar and weird animals, each verse illustrated by the author's own drawings. 24 drawings in 2 colors; 24 additional drawings. vii + 95pp. 6½ x 6. 21647-0 Paperbound $1.00

THE BROWNIES: THEIR BOOK, *Palmer Cox*
The book that made the Brownies a household word. Generations of readers have enjoyed the antics, predicaments and adventures of these jovial sprites, who emerge from the forest at night to play or to come to the aid of a deserving human. Delightful illustrations by the author decorate nearly every page. 24 short verse tales with 266 illustrations. 155pp. 6⅝ x 9¼.
21265-3 Paperbound $1.50

THE PRINCIPLES OF PSYCHOLOGY,
William James
The full long-course, unabridged, of one of the great classics of Western literature and science. Wonderfully lucid descriptions of human mental activity, the stream of thought, consciousness, time perception, memory, imagination, emotions, reason, abnormal phenomena, and similar topics. Original contributions are integrated with the work of such men as Berkeley, Binet, Mills, Darwin, Hume, Kant, Royce, Schopenhauer, Spinoza, Locke, Descartes, Galton, Wundt, Lotze, Herbart, Fechner, and scores of others. All contrasting interpretations of mental phenomena are examined in detail—introspective analysis, philosophical interpretation, and experimental research. "A classic," *Journal of Consulting Psychology.* "The main lines are as valid as ever," *Psychoanalytical Quarterly.* "Standard reading . . . a classic of interpretation," *Psychiatric Quarterly.* 94 illustrations. 1408pp. 5⅜ x 8.
20381-6, 20382-4 Two volume set, paperbound $6.00

VISUAL ILLUSIONS: THEIR CAUSES, CHARACTERISTICS AND APPLICATIONS,
M. Luckiesh
"Seeing is deceiving," asserts the author of this introduction to virtually every type of optical illusion known. The text both describes and explains the principles involved in color illusions, figure-ground, distance illusions, etc. 100 photographs, drawings and diagrams prove how easy it is to fool the sense: circles that aren't round, parallel lines that seem to bend, stationary figures that seem to move as you stare at them — illustration after illustration strains our credulity at what we see. Fascinating book from many points of view, from applications for artists, in camouflage, etc. to the psychology of vision. New introduction by William Ittleson, Dept. of Psychology, Queens College. Index. Bibliography. xxi + 252pp. 5⅜ x 8½. 21530-X Paperbound $1.50

FADS AND FALLACIES IN THE NAME OF SCIENCE,
Martin Gardner
This is the standard account of various cults, quack systems, and delusions which have masqueraded as science: hollow earth fanatics. Reich and orgone sex energy, dianetics, Atlantis, multiple moons, Forteanism, flying saucers, medical fallacies like iridiagnosis, zone therapy, etc. A new chapter has been added on Bridey Murphy, psionics, and other recent manifestations in this field. This is a fair, reasoned appraisal of eccentric theory which provides excellent inoculation against cleverly masked nonsense. "Should be read by everyone, scientist and non-scientist alike," R. T. Birge, Prof. Emeritus of Physics, Univ. of California; Former President, American Physical Society. Index. x + 365pp. 5⅜ x 8. 20394-8 Paperbound $2.00

ILLUSIONS AND DELUSIONS OF THE SUPERNATURAL AND THE OCCULT,
D. H. Rawcliffe
Holds up to rational examination hundreds of persistent delusions including crystal gazing, automatic writing, table turning, mediumistic trances, mental healing, stigmata, lycanthropy, live burial, the Indian Rope Trick, spiritualism, dowsing, telepathy, clairvoyance, ghosts, ESP, etc. The author explains and exposes the mental and physical deceptions involved, making this not only an exposé of supernatural phenomena, but a valuable exposition of characteristic types of abnormal psychology. Originally titled "The Psychology of the Occult." 14 illustrations. Index. 551pp. 5⅜ x 8. 20503-7 Paperbound $3.50

FAIRY TALE COLLECTIONS, *edited by Andrew Lang*
Andrew Lang's fairy tale collections make up the richest shelf-full of traditional children's stories anywhere available. Lang supervised the translation of stories from all over the world—familiar European tales collected by Grimm, animal stories from Negro Africa, myths of primitive Australia, stories from Russia, Hungary, Iceland, Japan, and many other countries. Lang's selection of translations are unusually high; many authorities consider that the most familiar tales find their best versions in these volumes. All collections are richly decorated and illustrated by H. J. Ford and other artists.

THE BLUE FAIRY BOOK. 37 stories. 138 illustrations. ix + 390pp. 5⅜ x 8½.
21437-0 Paperbound $1.95

THE GREEN FAIRY BOOK. 42 stories. 100 illustrations. xiii + 366pp. 5⅜ x 8½.
21439-7 Paperbound $1.75

THE BROWN FAIRY BOOK. 32 stories. 50 illustrations, 8 in color. xii + 350pp. 5⅜ x 8½.
21438-9 Paperbound $1.95

THE BEST TALES OF HOFFMANN, *edited by E. F. Bleiler*
10 stories by E. T. A. Hoffmann, one of the greatest of all writers of fantasy. The tales include "The Golden Flower Pot," "Automata," "A New Year's Eve Adventure," "Nutcracker and the King of Mice," "Sand-Man," and others. Vigorous characterizations of highly eccentric personalities, remarkably imaginative situations, and intensely fast pacing has made these tales popular all over the world for 150 years. Editor's introduction. 7 drawings by Hoffmann. xxxiii + 419pp. 5⅜ x 8½.
21793-0 Paperbound $2.25

GHOST AND HORROR STORIES OF AMBROSE BIERCE,
edited by E. F. Bleiler
Morbid, eerie, horrifying tales of possessed poets, shabby aristocrats, revived corpses, and haunted malefactors. Widely acknowledged as the best of their kind between Poe and the moderns, reflecting their author's inner torment and bitter view of life. Includes "Damned Thing," "The Middle Toe of the Right Foot," "The Eyes of the Panther," "Visions of the Night," "Moxon's Master," and over a dozen others. Editor's introduction. xxii + 199pp. 5⅜ x 8½.
20767-6 Paperbound $1.50

THREE GOTHIC NOVELS, *edited by E. F. Bleiler*
Originators of the still popular Gothic novel form, influential in ushering in early 19th-century Romanticism. Horace Walpole's *Castle of Otranto*, William Beckford's *Vathek*, John Polidori's *The Vampyre*, and a *Fragment* by Lord Byron are enjoyable as exciting reading or as documents in the history of English literature. Editor's introduction. xi + 291pp. 5⅜ x 8½.
21232-7 Paperbound $2.00

BEST GHOST STORIES OF LEFANU, *edited by E. F. Bleiler*
Though admired by such critics as V. S. Pritchett, Charles Dickens and Henry James, ghost stories by the Irish novelist Joseph Sheridan LeFanu have never become as widely known as his detective fiction. About half of the 16 stories in this collection have never before been available in America. Collection includes "Carmilla" (perhaps the best vampire story ever written), "The Haunted Baronet," "The Fortunes of Sir Robert Ardagh," and the classic "Green Tea." Editor's introduction. 7 contemporary illustrations. Portrait of LeFanu. xii + 467pp. 5⅜ x 8.
20415-4 Paperbound $2.50

EASY-TO-DO ENTERTAINMENTS AND DIVERSIONS WITH COINS, CARDS, STRING, PAPER AND MATCHES, *R. M. Abraham*
Over 300 tricks, games and puzzles will provide young readers with absorbing fun. Sections on card games; paper-folding; tricks with coins, matches and pieces of string; games for the agile; toy-making from common household objects; mathematical recreations; and 50 miscellaneous pastimes. Anyone in charge of groups of youngsters, including hard-pressed parents, and in need of suggestions on how to keep children sensibly amused and quietly content will find this book indispensable. Clear, simple text, copious number of delightful line drawings and illustrative diagrams. Originally titled "Winter Nights' Entertainments." Introduction by Lord Baden Powell. 329 illustrations. v + 186pp. 5⅜ x 8½. 20921-0 Paperbound $1.00

AN INTRODUCTION TO CHESS MOVES AND TACTICS SIMPLY EXPLAINED, *Leonard Barden*
Beginner's introduction to the royal game. Names, possible moves of the pieces, definitions of essential terms, how games are won, etc. explained in 30-odd pages. With this background you'll be able to sit right down and play. Balance of book teaches strategy — openings, middle game, typical endgame play, and suggestions for improving your game. A sample game is fully analyzed. True middle-level introduction, teaching you all the essentials without oversimplifying or losing you in a maze of detail. 58 figures. 102pp. 5⅜ x 8½. 21210-6 Paperbound $1.25

LASKER'S MANUAL OF CHESS, *Dr. Emanuel Lasker*
Probably the greatest chess player of modern times, Dr. Emanuel Lasker held the world championship 28 years, independent of passing schools or fashions. This unmatched study of the game, chiefly for intermediate to skilled players, analyzes basic methods, combinations, position play, the aesthetics of chess, dozens of different openings, etc., with constant reference to great modern games. Contains a brilliant exposition of Steinitz's important theories. Introduction by Fred Reinfeld. Tables of Lasker's tournament record. 3 indices. 308 diagrams. 1 photograph. xxx + 349pp. 5⅜ x 8. 20640-8 Paperbound $2.50

COMBINATIONS: THE HEART OF CHESS, *Irving Chernev*
Step-by-step from simple combinations to complex, this book, by a well-known chess writer, shows you the intricacies of pins, counter-pins, knight forks, and smothered mates. Other chapters show alternate lines of play to those taken in actual championship games; boomerang combinations; classic examples of brilliant combination play by Nimzovich, Rubinstein, Tarrasch, Botvinnik, Alekhine and Capablanca. Index. 356 diagrams. ix + 245pp. 5⅜ x 8½. 21744-2 Paperbound $2.00

HOW TO SOLVE CHESS PROBLEMS, *K. S. Howard*
Full of practical suggestions for the fan or the beginner — who knows only the moves of the chessmen. Contains preliminary section and 58 two-move, 46 three-move, and 8 four-move problems composed by 27 outstanding American problem creators in the last 30 years. Explanation of all terms and exhaustive index. "Just what is wanted for the student," Brian Harley. 112 problems, solutions. vi + 171pp. 5⅜ x 8. 20748-X Paperbound $1.50

SOCIAL THOUGHT FROM LORE TO SCIENCE,
H. E. Barnes and H. Becker
An immense survey of sociological thought and ways of viewing, studying, planning, and reforming society from earliest times to the present. Includes thought on society of preliterate peoples, ancient non-Western cultures, and every great movement in Europe, America, and modern Japan. Analyzes hundreds of great thinkers: Plato, Augustine, Bodin, Vico, Montesquieu, Herder, Comte, Marx, etc. Weighs the contributions of utopians, sophists, fascists and communists; economists, jurists, philosophers, ecclesiastics, and every 19th and 20th century school of scientific sociology, anthropology, and social psychology throughout the world. Combines topical, chronological, and regional approaches, treating the evolution of social thought as a process rather than as a series of mere topics. "Impressive accuracy, competence, and discrimination . . . easily the best single survey," *Nation*. Thoroughly revised, with new material up to 1960. 2 indexes. Over 2200 bibliographical notes. Three volume set. Total of 1586pp. 5⅜ x 8.
20901-6, 20902-4, 20903-2 Three volume set, paperbound $9.00

A HISTORY OF HISTORICAL WRITING, *Harry Elmer Barnes*
Virtually the only adequate survey of the whole course of historical writing in a single volume. Surveys developments from the beginnings of historiography in the ancient Near East and the Classical World, up through the Cold War. Covers major historians in detail, shows interrelationship with cultural background, makes clear individual contributions, evaluates and estimates importance; also enormously rich upon minor authors and thinkers who are usually passed over. Packed with scholarship and learning, clear, easily written. Indispensable to every student of history. Revised and enlarged up to 1961. Index and bibliography. xv + 442pp. 5⅜ x 8½.
20104-X Paperbound $2.75

JOHANN SEBASTIAN BACH, *Philipp Spitta*
The complete and unabridged text of the definitive study of Bach. Written some 70 years ago, it is still unsurpassed for its coverage of nearly all aspects of Bach's life and work. There could hardly be a finer non-technical introduction to Bach's music than the detailed, lucid analyses which Spitta provides for hundreds of individual pieces. 26 solid pages are devoted to the B minor mass, for example, and 30 pages to the glorious St. Matthew Passion. This monumental set also includes a major analysis of the music of the 18th century: Buxtehude, Pachelbel, etc. "Unchallenged as the last word on one of the supreme geniuses of music," John Barkham, *Saturday Review Syndicate*. Total of 1819pp. Heavy cloth binding. 5⅜ x 8.
22278-0, 22279-9 Two volume set, clothbound $15.00

BEETHOVEN AND HIS NINE SYMPHONIES, *George Grove*
In this modern middle-level classic of musicology Grove not only analyzes all nine of Beethoven's symphonies very thoroughly in terms of their musical structure, but also discusses the circumstances under which they were written, Beethoven's stylistic development, and much other background material. This is an extremely rich book, yet very easily followed; it is highly recommended to anyone seriously interested in music. Over 250 musical passages. Index. viii + 407pp. 5⅜ x 8.
20334-4 Paperbound $2.25

THREE SCIENCE FICTION NOVELS,
John Taine
Acknowledged by many as the best SF writer of the 1920's, Taine (under the name Eric Temple Bell) was also a Professor of Mathematics of considerable renown. Reprinted here are *The Time Stream*, generally considered Taine's best, *The Greatest Game*, a biological-fiction novel, and *The Purple Sapphire*, involving a supercivilization of the past. Taine's stories tie fantastic narratives to frameworks of original and logical scientific concepts. Speculation is often profound on such questions as the nature of time, concept of entropy, cyclical universes, etc. 4 contemporary illustrations. v + 532pp. 5⅜ x 8⅜.
21180-0 Paperbound $2.50

SEVEN SCIENCE FICTION NOVELS,
H. G. Wells
Full unabridged texts of 7 science-fiction novels of the master. Ranging from biology, physics, chemistry, astronomy, to sociology and other studies, Mr. Wells extrapolates whole worlds of strange and intriguing character. "One will have to go far to match this for entertainment, excitement, and sheer pleasure . . ."*New York Times.* Contents: The Time Machine, The Island of Dr. Moreau, The First Men in the Moon, The Invisible Man, The War of the Worlds, The Food of the Gods, In The Days of the Comet. 1015pp. 5⅜ x 8.
20264-X Clothbound $5.00

28 SCIENCE FICTION STORIES OF H. G. WELLS.
Two full, unabridged novels, *Men Like Gods* and *Star Begotten*, plus 26 short stories by the master science-fiction writer of all time! Stories of space, time, invention, exploration, futuristic adventure. Partial contents: *The Country of the Blind, In the Abyss, The Crystal Egg, The Man Who Could Work Miracles, A Story of Days to Come, The Empire of the Ants, The Magic Shop, The Valley of the Spiders, A Story of the Stone Age, Under the Knife, Sea Raiders,* etc. An indispensable collection for the library of anyone interested in science fiction adventure. 928pp. 5⅜ x 8.
20265-8 Clothbound $5.00

THREE MARTIAN NOVELS,
Edgar Rice Burroughs
Complete, unabridged reprinting, in one volume, of Thuvia, Maid of Mars; Chessmen of Mars; The Master Mind of Mars. Hours of science-fiction adventure by a modern master storyteller. Reset in large clear type for easy reading. 16 illustrations by J. Allen St. John. vi + 490pp. 5⅜ x 8½.
20039-6 Paperbound $2.50

AN INTELLECTUAL AND CULTURAL HISTORY OF THE WESTERN WORLD,
Harry Elmer Barnes
Monumental 3-volume survey of intellectual development of Europe from primitive cultures to the present day. Every significant product of human intellect traced through history: art, literature, mathematics, physical sciences, medicine, music, technology, social sciences, religions, jurisprudence, education, etc. Presentation is lucid and specific, analyzing in detail specific discoveries, theories, literary works, and so on. Revised (1965) by recognized scholars in specialized fields under the direction of Prof. Barnes. Revised bibliography. Indexes. 24 illustrations. Total of xxix + 1318pp.
21275-0, 21276-9, 21277-7 Three volume set, paperbound $8.25

HEAR ME TALKIN' TO YA, *edited by Nat Shapiro and Nat Hentoff*
In their own words, Louis Armstrong, King Oliver, Fletcher Henderson, Bunk
Johnson, Bix Beiderbecke, Billy Holiday, Fats Waller, Jelly Roll Morton,
Duke Ellington, and many others comment on the origins of jazz in New
Orleans and its growth in Chicago's South Side, Kansas City's jam sessions,
Depression Harlem, and the modernism of the West Coast schools. Taken
from taped conversations, letters, magazine articles, other first-hand sources.
Editors' introduction. xvi + 429pp. 5⅜ x 8½.   21726-4 Paperbound $2.00

THE JOURNAL OF HENRY D. THOREAU
A 25-year record by the great American observer and critic, as complete a
record of a great man's inner life as is anywhere available. Thoreau's Journals
served him as raw material for his formal pieces, as a place where he could
develop his ideas, as an outlet for his interests in wild life and plants, in
writing as an art, in classics of literature, Walt Whitman and other contemporaries, in politics, slavery, individual's relation to the State, etc. The
Journals present a portrait of a remarkable man, and are an observant social
history. Unabridged republication of 1906 edition, Bradford Torrey and
Francis H. Allen, editors. Illustrations. Total of 1888pp. 8⅜ x 12¼.
                     20312-3, 20313-1 Two volume set, clothbound $30.00

A SHAKESPEARIAN GRAMMAR, *E. A. Abbott*
Basic reference to Shakespeare and his contemporaries, explaining through
thousands of quotations from Shakespeare, Jonson, Beaumont and Fletcher,
North's *Plutarch* and other sources the grammatical usage differing from the
modern. First published in 1870 and written by a scholar who spent much of
his life isolating principles of Elizabethan language, the book is unlikely ever
to be superseded. Indexes. xxiv + 511pp. 5⅜ x 8½. 21582-2 Paperbound $3.00

FOLK-LORE OF SHAKESPEARE, *T. F. Thistelton Dyer*
Classic study, drawing from Shakespeare a large body of references to supernatural beliefs, terminology of falcony and hunting, games and sports, good
luck charms, marriage customs, folk medicines, superstitions about plants,
animals, birds, argot of the underworld, sexual slang of London, proverbs,
drinking customs, weather lore, and much else. From full compilation comes
a mirror of the 17th-century popular mind. Index. ix + 526pp. 5⅜ x 8½.
                                        21614-4 Paperbound $2.75

THE NEW VARIORUM SHAKESPEARE, *edited by H. H. Furness*
By far the richest editions of the plays ever produced in any country or
language. Each volume contains complete text (usually First Folio) of the
play, all variants in Quarto and other Folio texts, editorial changes by every
major editor to Furness's own time (1900), footnotes to obscure references or
language, extensive quotes from literature of Shakespearian criticism, essays
on plot sources (often reprinting sources in full), and much more.

HAMLET, *edited by H. H. Furness*
Total of xxvi + 905pp. 5⅜ x 8½.
                     21004-9, 21005-7 Two volume set, paperbound $5.25
TWELFTH NIGHT, *edited by H. H. Furness*
Index. xxii + 434pp. 5⅜ x 8½.   21189-4 Paperbound $2.75

LA BOHEME BY GIACOMO PUCCINI,
translated and introduced by Ellen H. Bleiler
Complete handbook for the operagoer, with everything needed for full enjoyment except the musical score itself. Complete Italian libretto, with new, modern English line-by-line translation—the only libretto printing all repeats; biography of Puccini; the librettists; background to the opera, Murger's La Boheme, etc.; circumstances of composition and performances; plot summary; and pictorial section of 73 illustrations showing Puccini, famous singers and performances, etc. Large clear type for easy reading. 124pp. 5⅜ x 8½.
20404-9 Paperbound $1.25

ANTONIO STRADIVARI: HIS LIFE AND WORK (1644-1737),
W. Henry Hill, Arthur F. Hill, and Alfred E. Hill
Still the only book that really delves into life and art of the incomparable Italian craftsman, maker of the finest musical instruments in the world today. The authors, expert violin-makers themselves, discuss Stradivari's ancestry, his construction and finishing techniques, distinguished characteristics of many of his instruments and their locations. Included, too, is story of introduction of his instruments into France, England, first revelation of their supreme merit, and information on his labels, number of instruments made, prices, mystery of ingredients of his varnish, tone of pre-1684 Stradivari violin and changes between 1684 and 1690. An extremely interesting, informative account for all music lovers, from craftsman to concert-goer. Republication of original (1902) edition. New introduction by Sydney Beck, Head of Rare Book and Manuscript Collections, Music Division, New York Public Library. Analytical index by Rembert Wurlitzer. Appendixes. 68 illustrations. 30 full-page plates. 4 in color. xxvi + 315pp. 5⅜ x 8½.
20425-1 Paperbound $2.25

MUSICAL AUTOGRAPHS FROM MONTEVERDI TO HINDEMITH,
Emanuel Winternitz
For beauty, for intrinsic interest, for perspective on the composer's personality, for subtleties of phrasing, shading, emphasis indicated in the autograph but suppressed in the printed score, the mss. of musical composition are fascinating documents which repay close study in many different ways. This 2-volume work reprints facsimiles of mss. by virtually every major composer, and many minor figures—196 examples in all. A full text points out what can be learned from mss., analyzes each sample. Index. Bibliography. 18 figures. 196 plates. Total of 170pp. of text. 7⅞ x 10¾.
21312-9, 21313-7 Two volume set, paperbound $5.00

J. S. BACH,
Albert Schweitzer
One of the few great full-length studies of Bach's life and work, and the study upon which Schweitzer's renown as a musicologist rests. On first appearance (1911), revolutionized Bach performance. The only writer on Bach to be musicologist, performing musician, and student of history, theology and philosophy, Schweitzer contributes particularly full sections on history of German Protestant church music, theories on motivic pictorial representations in vocal music, and practical suggestions for performance. Translated by Ernest Newman. Indexes. 5 illustrations. 650 musical examples. Total of xix + 928pp. 5⅜ x 8½.
21631-4, 21632-2 Two volume set, paperbound $4.50

THE METHODS OF ETHICS, *Henry Sidgwick*
Propounding no organized system of its own, study subjects every major methodological approach to ethics to rigorous, objective analysis. Study discusses and relates ethical thought of Plato, Aristotle, Bentham, Clarke, Butler, Hobbes, Hume, Mill, Spencer, Kant, and dozens of others. Sidgwick retains conclusions from each system which follow from ethical premises, rejecting the faulty. Considered by many in the field to be among the most important treatises on ethical philosophy. Appendix. Index. xlvii + 528pp. 5⅜ x 8½.
21608-X Paperbound $2.50

TEUTONIC MYTHOLOGY, *Jakob Grimm*
A milestone in Western culture; the work which established on a modern basis the study of history of religions and comparative religions. 4-volume work assembles and interprets everything available on religious and folkloristic beliefs of Germanic people (including Scandinavians, Anglo-Saxons, etc.). Assembling material from such sources as Tacitus, surviving Old Norse and Icelandic texts, archeological remains, folktales, surviving superstitions, comparative traditions, linguistic analysis, etc. Grimm explores pagan deities, heroes, folklore of nature, religious practices, and every other area of pagan German belief. To this day, the unrivaled, definitive, exhaustive study. Translated by J. S. Stallybrass from 4th (1883) German edition. Indexes. Total of lxxvii + 1887pp. 5⅜ x 8½.
21602-0, 21603-9, 21604-7, 21605-5 Four volume set, paperbound $11.00

THE I CHING, *translated by James Legge*
Called "The Book of Changes" in English, this is one of the Five Classics edited by Confucius, basic and central to Chinese thought. Explains perhaps the most complex system of divination known, founded on the theory that all things happening at any one time have characteristic features which can be isolated and related. Significant in Oriental studies, in history of religions and philosophy, and also to Jungian psychoanalysis and other areas of modern European thought. Index. Appendixes. 6 plates. xxi + 448pp. 5⅜ x 8½.
21062-6 Paperbound $2.75

HISTORY OF ANCIENT PHILOSOPHY, *W. Windelband*
One of the clearest, most accurate comprehensive surveys of Greek and Roman philosophy. Discusses ancient philosophy in general, intellectual life in Greece in the 7th and 6th centuries B.C., Thales, Anaximander, Anaximenes, Heraclitus, the Eleatics, Empedocles, Anaxagoras, Leucippus, the Pythagoreans, the Sophists, Socrates, Democritus (20 pages), Plato (50 pages), Aristotle (70 pages), the Peripatetics, Stoics, Epicureans, Sceptics, Neo-platonists, Christian Apologists, etc. 2nd German edition translated by H. E. Cushman. xv + 393pp. 5⅜ x 8.
20357-3 Paperbound $2.25

THE PALACE OF PLEASURE, *William Painter*
Elizabethan versions of Italian and French novels from *The Decameron,* Cinthio, Straparola, Queen Margaret of Navarre, and other continental sources — the very work that provided Shakespeare and dozens of his contemporaries with many of their plots and sub-plots and, therefore, justly considered one of the most influential books in all English literature. It is also a book that any reader will still enjoy. Total of cviii + 1,224pp.
21691-8, 21692-6, 21693-4 Three volume set, paperbound $6.75

THE WONDERFUL WIZARD OF OZ, *L. F. Baum*
All the original W. W. Denslow illustrations in full color—as much a part of
"The Wizard" as Tenniel's drawings are of "Alice in Wonderland." "The
Wizard" is still America's best-loved fairy tale, in which, as the author expresses
it, "The wonderment and joy are retained and the heartaches and nightmares
left out." Now today's young readers can enjoy every word and wonderful picture of the original book. New introduction by Martin Gardner. A Baum
bibliography. 23 full-page color plates. viii + 268pp. 5⅜ x 8.
20691-2 Paperbound $1.95

THE MARVELOUS LAND OF OZ, *L. F. Baum*
This is the equally enchanting sequel to the "Wizard," continuing the adventures of the Scarecrow and the Tin Woodman. The hero this time is a little
boy named Tip, and all the delightful Oz magic is still present. This is the
Oz book with the Animated Saw-Horse, the Woggle-Bug, and Jack Pumpkin-
head. All the original John R. Neill illustrations, 10 in full color. 287pp.
5⅜ x 8.   20692-0 Paperbound $1.75

ALICE'S ADVENTURES UNDER GROUND, *Lewis Carroll*
The original *Alice in Wonderland*, hand-lettered and illustrated by Carroll
himself, and originally presented as a Christmas gift to a child-friend. Adults
as well as children will enjoy this charming volume, reproduced faithfully
in this Dover edition. While the story is essentially the same, there are slight
changes, and Carroll's spritely drawings present an intriguing alternative to
the famous Tenniel illustrations. One of the most popular books in Dover's
catalogue. Introduction by Martin Gardner. 38 illustrations. 128pp. 5⅜ x 8½.
21482-6 Paperbound $1.00

THE NURSERY "ALICE," *Lewis Carroll*
While most of us consider *Alice in Wonderland* a story for children of all
ages, Carroll himself felt it was beyond younger children. He therefore provided this simplified version, illustrated with the famous Tenniel drawings
enlarged and colored in delicate tints, for children aged "from Nought to
Five." Dover's edition of this now rare classic is a faithful copy of the 1889
printing, including 20 illustrations by Tenniel, and front and back covers
reproduced in full color. Introduction by Martin Gardner. xxiii + 67pp.
6⅛ x 9¼.   21610-1 Paperbound $1.75

THE STORY OF KING ARTHUR AND HIS KNIGHTS, *Howard Pyle*
A fast-paced, exciting retelling of the best known Arthurian legends for young
readers by one of America's best story tellers and illustrators. The sword
Excalibur, wooing of Guinevere, Merlin and his downfall, adventures of Sir
Pellias and Gawaine, and others. The pen and ink illustrations are vividly
imagined and wonderfully drawn. 41 illustrations. xviii + 313pp. 6⅛ x 9¼.
21445-1 Paperbound $2.00

Prices subject to change without notice.